Interdisciplinary Perspectives in Healthcare

Editors:

Brenda Freshman, PhD
Assistant Professor
Health Care Administration Department
California State University, Long Beach

Louis Rubino, PhD, FACHE
Professor/Program Director
Health Administration Program
California State University, Northridge

Yolanda (Linda) Reid Chassiakos, MD, FAAP
Clinical Assistant Professor, Pediatrics
David Geffen School of Medicine
University of California, Los Angeles
Director, Klotz Student Health Center
California State University, Northridge

JONES & BARTLETT
LEARNING

World Headquarters
Jones & Bartlett Learning
40 Tall Pine Drive
Sudbury, MA 01776
978-443-5000
info@jblearning.com
www.jblearning.com

Jones & Bartlett Learning Canada
6339 Ormindale Way
Mississauga, ON L5V 1J2
Canada

Jones & Bartlett Learning International
Barb House, Barb Mews
London W6 7PA
United Kingdom

Jones & Bartlett Learning books and products are available through most bookstores and online booksellers. To contact Jones & Bartlett Learning directly, call 800-832-0034, fax 978-443-8000, or visit our website at www.jblearning.com.

Substantial discounts on bulk quantities of Jones & Bartlett Learning publications are available to corporations, professional associations, and other qualified organizations. For details and specific discount information, contact the special sales department at Jones & Bartlett Learning via the above contact information or send an email to specialsales@jblearning.com.

Production Credits
Publisher: Michael Brown
Production Director: Amy Rose
Associate Editor: Katey Birtcher
Editorial Assistant: Catie Heverling
Senior Production Editor: Tracey Chapman
Production Assistant: Roya Millard
Marketing Manager: Sophie Fleck
Manufacturing and Inventory Control Supervisor: Amy Bacus
Composition: Publishers' Design and Production Services, Inc.
Cover Design: Scott Moden
Printing and Binding: Malloy, Inc.
Cover image: Clockwise from top: © AbelStock; © Photos.com; © Photos.com; © Photodisc; back cover: © Andresr/ShutterStock, Inc.
Cover Printing: Malloy, Inc.

Library of Congress Cataloging-in-Publication Data
Collaboration across the disciplines in health care / [edited by] Brenda Freshman, Louis Rubino, Yolanda Reid Chassiakos.
p. ; cm.
Includes bibliographical references.
ISBN 978-0-7637-5558-4 (pbk.)
1. Health care teams. I. Freshman, Brenda. II. Rubino, Louis. III. Chassiakos, Yolanda Reid. [DNLM: 1. Patient Care Team—organization & administration. 2. Cooperative Behavior. 3. Interprofessional Relations. W 84.8 C697 2010]
R729.5.H4C65 2010
610.69—dc22

2008050237

ISBN: 978-1-4496-0084-6

6048

Printed in the United States of America
14 13 12 11 10 10 9 8 7 6 5 4 3 2 1

Contents

CHAPTER 1

The Health Care Team Members: Who Are They and What Do They Do?

Paul R. Torrens, MD, MPH

LEARNING OBJECTIVES

After completing this chapter, the reader will be able to:

1. Describe the importance of multidisciplinary teams as the primary vehicle for collaboration in health care.
2. Identify the specific healthcare professionals involved in a healthcare team and their professional roles.
3. Identify the main team functions that are necessary for the successful operation of any healthcare team collaboration.
4. Identify which healthcare professionals carry out which health team functions.
5. Describe key factors in designing future healthcare teams such as selection of team members as guided by team functions and goals.

KEY TERMS

Healthcare teams
Collaborative efforts in health care
Team member designations by healthcare profession

Team member designations by team function
Intrateam/interteam communication
Professional interactions

INTRODUCTION

In its landmark report, *Crossing in the Quality Chasm: A New Health System for the 21st Century* (Committee on Quality, 2001), the Institute of Medicine of the National Academy of Sciences described the explosion of new scientific knowledge in all aspects of health care and suggested that "Making use of new knowledge may require that health professionals develop new skills or that their roles change." The report went on to say that "Incorporating new knowledge requires skilled leadership to engage the participation of health professionals in collaborative teams," and that "What is sometimes thought to be collaboration, may be in fact be uncoordinated or sequential action rather than collaborative work." To have effective collaboration, the report suggests that "Effective working teams must be created and maintained," but points out that "members of teams are typically trained in separate disciplines and educational settings, leaving them unprepared to practice in complex collaborative settings." The report also stated "The work of each individual may be efficient from the perspective of his or her own tasks, but overall the efforts are suboptimal and may not serve the needs of patients"(Committee on Quality, 2001).

The purpose of this chapter is to examine the individual professional contributions to healthcare teams and to describe the functions that must be carried out to allow healthcare teams to work effectively, so that the maximum benefit to patients can be obtained.

CASE STUDY: A 43-YEAR-OLD MOTHER WITH EARLY STAGE BREAST CANCER

Linda Simmons (*name has been changed*) is a 43-year-old previously healthy woman, and wife and mother of two girls, ages 8 and 10. During the course of her regular breast self-examination, she discovered a suspicious lump in her left breast. She went to her family physician whose examination confirmed the presence of a suspicious mass. Her physician confirmed the diagnosis after Mrs. Simmons obtained a mammogram at the local hospital. Mrs. Simmons was then referred to a surgical oncologist on the staff of a cancer center at a nearby teaching hospital who carried out a surgical biopsy. The biopsy revealed a localized early stage malignancy of the breast. The surgeon immediately brought in a medical oncologist and, together with the occasional involvement of a radiation therapist at the hospital, they developed a tentative treatment plan involving limited breast surgery, medical chemotherapy, and possible follow-up radiation therapy.

Mrs. Simmons was admitted to the hospital and the recommended surgery was carried out. This was followed by a course of chemotherapy over several months that involved regular visits to the medical oncologist's office for administration of the appropriate medication. Because Mrs. Simmons had had previous bouts of clinical depression and was showing signs of a possible repeat episode of depression as a result of her diagnosis and treatment, her family physician referred her to a mental health professional for possible intervention and medical treatment. Because the chemotherapy medicine was quite expensive and her husband's health insurance plan did not pay the full cost of treatment, Mrs. Simmons met with a social worker at the cancer center to see if there might be some way to offset the high costs of the proposed chemotherapy.

Throughout the course of treatment in the hospital and as an outpatient in the medical oncologist's office, Mrs. Simmons developed very close ties with the nurses who participated in various aspects of her care. Indeed, in both settings, Mrs. Simmons came to depend upon the nursing staff members for clinical services and, perhaps more importantly, for personal support and information. She believed that the nursing personnel were the strongest and most sustained durable link in her process of care.

At one point, a clinical pharmacist was consulted because the chemotherapy was having severe side effects of nausea and weakness, and a change of medication dosage was recommended; an additional new medication was ordered to relieve the side effects of the chemotherapy. Also, early in her treatment, Mrs. Simmons had a series of genetic tests to determine whether several specific breast cancer-related genes were present, because their presence or absence might influence the choice of chemotherapy. After discovery that she was positive for the presence of several of these genes, Mrs. Simmons was seen by a genetic counselor who explained the relevance of these findings to her care; this genetic counselor also helped her to review the appropriateness of testing her two daughters for these genes either now or at a later point in their lives.

At the present time, Mrs. Simmons has successfully completed her chemotherapy regime and is being followed as an outpatient by both the medical oncologist and her family physician, with occasional visits to the hospital for laboratory tests and x-rays. Fortunately, both physicians and the hospital maintain electronic medical record systems, but because they are not linked together into a single system, Mrs. Simmons must follow all three systems separately to get a complete picture of her care and prognosis. Her husband's health insurance carrier participates in a breast cancer case management program as well and has an electronic medical record system relating to her insurance-covered care, but Mrs. Simmons has found that less useful than the other three local systems.

MEMBERS OF THE HEALTH CARE TEAM BY PROFESSIONAL BACKGROUND

A review of Mrs. Simmons' medical care for her breast cancer suggests a very good standard of care, provided by a group of widely-varied health care professionals working together as a "team," sometimes in a formal fashion (during her inpatient hospital care, for example) and sometimes in a more informal, ad hoc way (during her care as an outpatient, for example). One way to better understand these "teams" and how they functioned is to examine the various members according to their professional backgrounds and professional designations to see how the individual professions contributed to the total process.

The first group of professionals was physicians, the professionals who had the responsibility for making important clinical decisions and carrying out many of those decisions in practice. However, within the general designation of "physicians" there were several subsets of the profession, each of which carried out different responsibilities and played different clinical roles.

Mrs. Simmons' family physician, for example, was the point of first contact for her when she realized that there might be a lump in her breast. This physician arranged the referrals to more specialized care and then served as a continuing point of contact and support for Mrs. Simmons, especially as the number of physicians involved in her care grew. This family physician provided Mrs. Simmons with a "medical home" before her illness, during her treatment, and after its completion.

The surgical oncologist provided specialized expertise in Mrs. Simmons' disease, brought in other medical specialists as needed, and also carried out direct interventions twice: once to conduct the surgical biopsy and once to carry out the surgical removal of the tumor itself. The medical oncologist provided expertise about appropriate chemotherapy and actually administered the chemotherapy itself over many months when that phase of treatment began. The radiation therapist provided specialized knowledge in his area of expertise when asked and would have provided the appropriate therapy itself if it had been decided to include it in this phase of her treatment. Although all of these professionals were "physicians," their professional backgrounds, training, and—more importantly—their roles in the overall treatment process were markedly different.

In addition to the physicians, many other healthcare professionals played a variety of essential roles as Mrs. Simmons' process of care unfolded. Without their involvement at the proper time and in the proper way, the best efforts of the physicians simply might not have had the maximum effect possible. Various laboratory and x-ray technicians assisted with important diagnostic procedures when necessary. The mental health professional, a clinical psychologist, took on an important role in the diagnosis and treatment of a possible depressive illness arising at least partially from the primary diagnosis and its treatment. When significant side effects developed during the course of chemotherapy, the clinical pharmacist was able to suggest ways to continue effective primary treatment and cope appropriately with the side effects of treatment when needed.

Mrs. Simmons' process of care also introduced two newer professional disciplines that will be increasingly important in the care of patients in the years ahead: the expert in clinical genetics and the expert in newer electronic information systems. The work of the clinical genetics expert has already been mentioned and was essential in two aspects of her care: assisting the medical oncologist in choosing the best course of chemotherapy by providing him with important genetic diagnostic information and assisting the patient to understand the role of genetics in breast cancer for herself, her daughters, and her other female relatives.

The services of the expert in electronic information systems were not overt and external in Mrs. Simmons' case, but their impact was present throughout all phases of her care. Providing high-quality medical care for patients with a serious illness is now a very complex matter, often involving a staggering amount of information to gather, process, and make data available to all who need it, including patients and their families. Health information technology and its management have become critical to the success of high quality, collaborative health services delivery.

Throughout the entire course of Mrs. Simmons' care, the one professional group that was continuously present and essential to the success of that care was the profession of nursing. At all stages of her care, a clinical nurse played a central part in keeping the process moving forward, delivering specific services and support, and providing the substance and structure of the entire caring process itself. Professional nurses were ubiquitous throughout her course of care. Without them, there simply would have been no unified process and direction for Mrs. Simmons' care.

It should be pointed out that there are also subsets within the nursing profession as there are with physicians. All nurses are not the same in what they do, nor do they fulfill the same roles as all other nurses; sometimes the differences in their individual roles are more important than their similarities. Mrs. Simmons, for example, encountered nurses in the operating theater, on the wards of the hospital postoperatively, and in the delivery of chemotherapy and follow-up care in the medical oncologist's office. All were in the same professional grouping, but each was fulfilling a different role.

It should be obvious from this brief summary of one patient's process of care that a wide variety of healthcare professionals is needed to provide high-quality health care today. As this care becomes increasingly complex and challenging, the proper "mix" of professional talents and resources becomes broader and broader, and the difficulty of putting together effective teams becomes greater. It is becoming increasingly apparent that the effort to produce high-quality care is not hampered by lack of clinical expertise in the individual professions but rather by lack of appropriate knowledge and experience among these groups as to how to make these multidisciplinary teams work well.

This lack of skill in making healthcare teams work well to some extent reflects badly on the early formative training of healthcare professionals in general. As a rule, each professional group, whether it is medicine, nursing, pharmacy, or any other group, trains the future members of their professions in their own professional enclaves. There is relatively little cross-training or interaction with the other professional groups with which a particular discipline must eventually work. There is also little transition or flow between and among the professional groups; the majority of the training time is spent in developing the unique skills necessary for one particular professional body. This results in professionals who are highly competent in the specifics of their own field and, at the same time, virtually unaware of the specifics of others. This lack of integration and exposure to the fields of others in early training leads to highly trained individuals in each professional group but poorly prepared members of interprofessional teams or collaborative groups.

To design better healthcare teams, the first steps are to identify the professional skills that are necessary to deliver the health team's ultimate product, and understand the cultures and values of the specific healthcare professional groups who can deliver the needed care. Understanding how each professional group works and what that group needs for the maximum effectiveness of its contributions is essential to creating effective collaboration in health care.

Successful health care collaboration also depends upon organizational structures (i.e. teams) that have rules and roles of their own. No amount of understanding and knowledge about the other professionals in a healthcare team will make a collaboration successful if the organization and structure of the team is flawed. Therefore, it is important to look at the organization of healthcare teams from the point of the organizational roles and functions within any effective healthcare team.

MEMBERS OF THE HEALTH CARE TEAM BY ROLE AND FUNCTION

Collaboration between and among health professionals usually takes place around team efforts of a formal or informal nature, particularly in the care of illnesses that are complex or chronic in nature. It involves interaction between and among different types of professionals and is enhanced when the members of a collaborative understand each others cultures, values, and methods.

Another way to understand healthcare collaboration is to view health care as a system or an organizational process that involves many different functions that must be accomplished if the overall process of care is to be maximally effective. This approach examines whether the key functions are specified and carried out and, if so, by which professionals. Analysis of collaboration from a systems perspective is as important as the understanding of the clinical roles played by each individual professional contributor.

What are the roles and functions that are important to identify in any collaborative team effort? There seem to be seven key functions that must be carried out in any effective team activity:

1. Process access/entry point/referral guide
2. Clinical leader/clinical decision maker
3. Technical expert/consultant
4. Support service(s) provider
5. Process coordinator/point of continuing contact

6. Resource manager/coordinator
7. Information coordinator/communicator

Not every healthcare collaboration requires all these individual roles and functions, but in those circumstances where the illness involved is serious, complex, or chronic in nature, these functions will certainly need to be considered.

Process Access/Entry Point/Referral Guide

The first step in seeking or obtaining care is to find an entry point to the needed healthcare process; then, if necessary, the patient and provider can move on to more elaborate and specialized points of service and care. Although in this age of improved and intensified communication there may not seem to be any challenges related to entering the healthcare process, entry in truth may be quite complicated. Lack of a usual healthcare provider or medical home, lack of financial resources or insurance coverage, and lack of language capacity of understanding, all can influence where, when, and how a person can enter into the healthcare process.

In Mrs. Simmons' case, when she first discovered a possible lump in her breast, she spoke with a female friend of hers who told her that a family relative had encountered a similar problem and had received care from a general surgeon in the community. Mrs. Simmons was told that, although this surgeon was not known as a cancer specialist, he was well-regarded as a general surgeon and had provided good care as far as she knew.

Because Mrs. Simmons had a good relationship with her family physician, a young female physician recently trained in family practice and specializing in women's health care, she related to her doctor how her friend had mentioned this general surgeon in the community. The family physician responded that she would be more comfortable if Mrs. Simmons sought surgical care at a nearby teaching hospital that had an organized cancer program. The doctor had referred several patients to a surgical oncologist there and had had good experiences with him. The physician's opinion was that the cancer program had a higher volume of breast cancer patients, offered a wider range of services, and generally had more expertise available for Mrs. Simmons' care.

The family physician related that she was also pleased with that particular surgical oncologist at the nearby teaching hospital because he always reported back to the referring physician in detail about his findings and about the progress of the case. The family physician mentioned that this was not always true with her referrals to other specialists. She believed it was important that she continued to be involved with Mrs. Simmons' care over the course of her illness. Mrs. Simmons was convinced to follow her family physician's recommendations.

However, other types of access/entry/referral points could be just as effective, if operated correctly. Mrs. Simmons' family physician described another successful entry. One of her patients was a child with a genetic condition whose parents had gone to one of the referral services sponsored by the national organization connected with this condition to find an expert in their local area. On the other hand, the doctor revealed that she also had patients who had gone online to unauthorized and unsupervised Web sites for information and possible referrals. These patients had found themselves inundated with high-pressure sales pitches for unauthorized, unproven, and possibly dangerous treatments and medications.

The access/entry/referral activity is a critical function for any collaborative team effort, because the point of entry may determine the eventual major source of care coordination and future care, and, to a great extent, the ultimate outcome of that care for the patient.

Clinical Leader(s)/Clinical Decision Makers

Mrs. Simmons was referred to an expert surgical oncologist who quickly involved a medical oncologist in her care. They had worked together on many occasions, had quite a good understanding of each other's roles, and had no problem in deferring to the other's opinion when it was appropriate. They continued to jointly manage the clinical aspects of Mrs. Simmons' care, with the surgical oncologist taking the major initiative early in the process and the medical oncologist taking the major role after the surgical interventions were carried out. Mrs. Simmons' family physician continued to keep track of her progress through her contact with the surgical oncologist and found him to be more communicative than the medical oncologist, although both responded well when she asked for follow-up reports. Unfortunately, this type of personal cooperation and close communication is seemingly less common in these days of extremely busy medical specialty practices. This is probably not due to any lack of interest in communication, but rather to increasingly busy schedules and demands on physicians' time.

There is occasional uncertainty about leadership in clinical collaborations that can be traced to the involvement of many specialists, each of whom believe (with some good reason) that they are experts in their particular area and should be actively consulted in the collaborative process. In Mrs. Simmons' case, no less than five clinical experts were directly involved in her care (the family physician, the surgical oncologist, the medical oncologist, the radiation therapist, and the clinical psychologist) and the situation could have easily led to confusion, conflict, and lack of coordination. Fortunately, it did not for this case because of the professional strengths of the two leading oncologists and their willingness to work together for a common purpose, as well as the established relationship with the family physician and her coordination and facilitation of communications.

The function of clinical decision-making and leadership is central to the entire collaborative team process, so the focus of that decision-making authority and responsibility should be clearly identified and recognized by all team members. As will be pointed out later, however, this does not mean that the clinical decision-maker(s) must also operate or manage all of the details of the team effort, as that management organizational role can perhaps be best done by others.

Technical Expert/Consultant

In any collaborative effort, a number of technical experts also may be involved, and their roles and functions are important to identify and integrate into the larger process. It is essential to plan how best to involve them in a timely and appropriate fashion and perhaps to actually assist them in their participation in the overall process.

In Mrs. Simmons' case, four technical experts or consultants were successfully brought in to deal with various aspects of her care and one additional expert was approached but could not be successfully included. The four successful consultants were the radiation therapist, the clinical psychologist, the clinical pharmacist, and the genetics counselor. The one unsuccessful involvement was a neurologist who was contacted to appraise some severe headaches that Mrs. Simmons was having during the course of her chemotherapy. Unfortunately, his office could not provide an appropriate appointment for almost a month and by that time, the headaches had subsided and the consultation was no longer thought to be necessary.

In any complex or chronic illness, not only are first-line clinical experts and decision-makers necessary, but usually there is a need for technical expertise and consultations about more limited and specialized aspects of care. Blending these specialized technical reviews and interventions into the overall care process can be difficult and sometimes damaging to the smooth and timely operation of the broader process; this can be facilitated by the medical home or care coordinator.

Support Service(s) Provider

Just as there is need for technical expertise and consultants in the collaborative team effort, frequently individual support services that enhance and expand the primary clinical services are necessary. These are services such as x-ray and laboratory, physical and occupational therapy, social work and social support services, home nursing care and long-term care, transportation services for the disabled, meals-on-wheels and other home assistance services, and support groups and individual counseling for patients and family members. These services are not aimed at the primary disease entity itself, but rather are focused on the damages and aftermath of the disease and its treatment.

In Mrs. Simmons' case, there was need for x-ray and laboratory services provided by the hospital, social work assistance in dealing with her prolonged absence from work and her possible job loss, and nutritional advice and supplements when her chemotherapy interfered with her usual food intake. She had been referred to and took an active part in a breast cancer survivor group sponsored by her local church, and she visited a physical therapist when she thought that some shoulder muscles were weaker after surgery and were hampering her ability to return to her previously active swimming routine.

Very often, in the heat of active treatment for the primary illness, these secondary support services are overlooked or underappreciated because they do not necessarily deal with urgent life and death matters. However Mrs. Simmons probably would be the first to say that the support of her church pastor and her breast cancer survivor group members were extremely important in helping her and her husband deal effectively with the stresses of her primary cancer treatment events.

Coordination of Effort/Point of Continuing Contact for Providers and Patients

It is clear that many healthcare professionals take part in any process of care, ranging from those who are continuously and intensely involved to those who play more of a "cameo" role, coming in as needed for a brief (and perhaps critical) technical role and then moving off the scene. Often there is no central point of coordination of all these efforts in an organizational (and not necessarily clinical) sense. From the patient's point of view, it also may be very difficult to keep track of the involvement of all the separate individual specialists as well as confusing to know where to go to get a complete picture of what is going on.

The role of organizational coordination of the efforts of all the individual team players therefore becomes critical and essential to the smooth functioning of the collaborative effort. The coordinator helps all those involved in the patient's care process to know what is happening, what is expected of them, and what their activities should be in relation to the activities of others. The organizational coordinator is not necessarily the clinical decision-maker, although clinical decision-makers can take on the coordination role if he, she, or they are willing and capable.

In Mrs. Simmons' case, this role was assumed by a staff member at the hospital's cancer program, where both the surgical oncologist and medical oncologist were on staff. In this well-organized cancer care program, there was a specific nonclinical person (designated a "care process coordinator") who served as the central point of contact for Mrs. Simmons and all her various clinical specialists. This care process coordinator was assigned to Mrs. Simmons' case early in the process and became responsible for making the patient's appointments with consultants, laboratory, and x-ray services as well as for ensuring that these appointments and all other aspects of Mrs. Simmons' care were proceeding smoothly. The coordinator was also the person who would retrieve any needed medical records or test reports, and who would remain the point of continuing contact for Mrs. Simmons and everyone else involved with her care.

Simply having a group of highly-skilled professionals working for the same patient does not guarantee an effective collaboration and team effort. The coordinator helps individual skills and services mesh together in an operational way that increases efficiency, quality, and patient and provider satisfaction. It is often a poorly recognized, underpaid, and underappreciated role and function, but it is central to effective and successful collaboration.

Resource Manager/Resource Coordinator

With the growing complexity of medical and hospital billing, health insurance requirements and processes, and economic pressures on both patients and providers in recent years, a new role has developed: the financial resources coordinator or manager. This role and function is often critical for patient's access to care, for the providers' reimbursement, and for all participants in the healthcare process to have some sense of satisfaction and peace of mind with regards to the economic aspects of health care.

In Mrs. Simmons' case, she was fortunate that she had adequate health insurance coverage through her husband's employer and initially believed that all her expenses would be covered by that plan. While it was true that most of her expenses were covered to some degree, it sometimes took considerable effort to get certain newer treatments and medications approved for treatment by the plan. Additionally, she and her husband had to pay a significant share of the total cost, and experienced confusion about what was owed.

In the past, Mrs. Simmons' financial issues probably would have been assigned to a billing clerk in the hospital's accounting office and to an office manager in the different physicians' offices. Each of these people dealt primarily with bills in their sector of health care and had little interest in the finances of any other areas of care, even though all the individual areas overlapped and interacted with all the others in many significant ways. In addition, each of these individuals was usually dealing with difficult matters (i.e. bill paying) and sometimes had bad news to give and unpleasant actions to take. These often difficult and unpleasant transactions were handled by staff who were completely untrained in dealing with people in a co-operative way, which led to the perception of the financial staff as the "bad guys" by both providers and patients.

In Mrs. Simmons case, the care process coordinator at the hospital's cancer center understood all the challenges of financing complex health care from her own personal family experience and she felt determined to do all she could to minimize the negative aspects of each patient's experience. Based on her own family's experience, she had often said, "It is bad enough that our patients have cancer; we should not handle the billing process in such a harsh and unpleasant way that it only makes matters worse."

As a result, she asked for permission to work with one specific billing clerk in the finance office and requested that they work together to handle all aspects of patient billing for all cancer center services. Whenever billing problems arose, either with the providers, patients, or insurance plans, this coordinator advised her patients and providers to call her or her colleague in the finance office and they would work together to find the best solution.

They were not always able to solve individual billing and financial problems, but they made it clear to patients and providers that solving billing and insurance issues were important parts of the cancer center's total program.

The important point here is that financial and insurance issues in health care are increasingly complex and difficult, and sometimes involve determining where and how patients receive care in a timely and supportive fashion. In any collaborative team effort around complex patient care, there is an important function of financial resource management that needs to be included in any good team process.

Information Coordinator/Communicator

A final important function for any collaborative team effort is the coordination and management of information from a wide variety of sources. It includes making that information available to the people for whom it has significance and importance, such as providers and patients.

In the past, information about a person's health care was gathered at a variety of sites and in a variety of ways. Its assemblage was often the result of random circumstances and opportunity, not intention. As a result, the information available to patients and providers was often located in many sites and separate information systems, was inadequate or incomplete, and was not easily viewed in its totality by anyone. Communication of this information was even more individual and opportunistic, and no participant in the healthcare collaboration could ever be sure that they had a complete and current picture of the case. As a result, tests and examinations were often repeated by each individual provider, so that each one would have the information at hand that he or she needed.

Information is a vital and even essential resource for the provision of excellent patient care. It should be complete, well-integrated into the patient's overall record, and easily available for review and discussion by multidisciplinary teams. The challenge is how best to make this wide variety of information and resources available to everyone who needs it in a timely and appropriate fashion. To perform this information coordination function effectively, this new professional role is still developing.

For the present, the information coordination role and function is played, not by an individual healthcare professional, but by an electronic medical record or, more correctly, by a series of electronic medical records kept by individual providers and institutions. The function is fulfilled not by one person who continuously reviews and updates an individual patient's complete health record, but by an information system specialist, usually at a distance. This professional assesses the effectiveness of the broader system beyond an individual patient record and determines whether important pieces of information have been entered in timely and accurate manners.

The creation of the care process coordinator role was valuable in Mrs. Simmons' case, because the coordinator was able to follow her care process and could intervene if needed information was not forthcoming. However, the care process coordinator is not an information systems specialist or expert, and cannot serve as an expert information coordinator and communicator. For that reason, this role and function will belong to a more active member of healthcare collaborative teams in the future.

In Mrs. Simmons' case, there was no central repository of all information relating to her illness and progress. To determine her complete picture, she had to access four separate electronic information systems and put their sometimes disparate information formats and items together for herself. This situation will be reduced in the near future to two separate systems, one for all hospital-connected physician and hospital services and one for her family physician. But in this case study, Mrs. Simmons still had to piece her record together on a day-to-day basis and serve as her own information system coordinator, relying on her connection with the care coordinator for those items of information that she could not find herself.

Table 1-1 presents an overview of the teams, roles, and functions involved in Mrs. Simmon's care.

CONCLUSION

All patient care involves some degree of collaboration and teamwork between and among individuals of various professions and disciplines. Not all interactions between healthcare personnel need to be considered as part of a formal team effort, because much of health care involves personal interactions taking place between only a few individuals on a one-time, short-term basis.

For more serious, more complex, and/or chronic illnesses and conditions, however, the model of collaborative team-related efforts becomes increasingly crucial to ensure efficient, effective, and high-quality care. The days of

Table 1-1. Mrs. Simmon's Case Example: Teams, Roles, and Functions

Team Member's Professional Area	**Roles and Functions**	**Case Example**
Clinical decision-maker	Leadership, manages clinical aspects of care	Family physician Surgical oncologist Medical oncologist Radiation therapist Clinical psychologist
Technical expert/ Consultant	Consultant, provides information about specialized aspects of care	Radiation therapist Clinical psychologist Clinical pharmacist Genetics counselor
Support services	Enhance, support, and expand the primary care services	X-ray Laboratory Physical therapy Occupational therapy Social work Social support services Home nursing care and other home services Long term care Transportation Support groups Counseling
Coordination point	Organizes all efforts; central point of setting timely appointments with appropriate specialists and other service providers	Care process coordinator
Resource manager	Handles the economic aspects of care	Care process coordinator Billing clerk
Information coordinator	Coordinates and manages information from a wide variety of sources	Electronic medical records Information specialist

an individual healthcare professional working alone or in a very small group are rapidly waning and are being replaced by organized multidisciplinary team efforts. Learning how to promote improved collaboration between and among various healthcare professionals and learning how to create and support capable healthcare teams are critical strategies for the long-term success and cost-effectiveness of modern health care.

The seminal report from the Institute of Medicine, *Crossing the Quality Chasm* quoted at the beginning of this chapter, provides a template for this evolution towards broad-based successful collaboration. The Committee on Quality of Health Care in America (2001) identified four characteristics of effective healthcare teams in the future:

> These characteristics include
> 1. team makeup, such as having appropriate size and composition and the ability to reduce negative effects of status differences between, for example, physicians and nurses;
> 2. team processes, such as communication structures, conflict management, and leadership that emphasizes excellence and conveys clear goals and expectations;
> 3. the nature of the team's tasks, such as matching roles and training to the level of complexity and promoting cohesiveness when work is highly interdependent; and
> 4. environmental context, such as obtaining needed resources and establishing appropriate rewards.

In review, two ways were presented of understanding the professions and the professionals who comprise today's (and tomorrow's) healthcare teams. One way is to understand the professions themselves: what they do, how they do it, and what they think about what they are doing. The other is to understand the roles and functions that need to be carried out in any team effort, quite separate from the individual professionals taking part. The first understanding focuses on healthcare professionals as individuals and as members of professional groups; the second understanding focuses on organizational structures—formal and informal—and what it takes to make them work. Consideration of both these points of view in collaborative facilitation will lead to improved care, higher quality, and lower costs over time, which is an important set of objectives for all healthcare professionals and consumers.

DISCUSSION QUESTIONS

1. Why is it important to understand health team members' professional backgrounds and their individual clinical roles in the collaborative healthcare process?
2. Why is it important to know the specific team functions that take place in healthcare teams and to know which healthcare professional is carrying them out?
3. How might individual health professions change their educational programs to better prepare their graduates for improved collaboration in the future?
4. How might you design healthcare teams to enhance and improve collaboration?

REFERENCE

Committee on Quality of Health Care in America, Institute of Medicine, National Academy of Sciences. (2001). *Crossing the Quality Chasm: A New Health System for the 21st Century*. Washington, DC: National Academy Press.

SUGGESTED READING

Barton, P.L. (2003). The Health Services workforce. In *Understanding the U.S. Health Services System* (2nd ed.). Washington, DC: Health Administration Press.

Mick, S., & White, K. (2008). Health care professionals. In S. Williams & P. Torrens (Eds.), *Introduction to Health Services* (7th ed.). Florence, KY: Thomson/Delmar Learning.

U.S. Department of Health and Human Services, Center for Disease Control and Prevention. (2007). *Health, United States, 2007* (with Chartbook on Trends in the Health of Americans, Tables 105–112, "Personnel"). Hyattsville, MD: National Center for Health Statistics.

CHAPTER 2

Leadership Development in the Interdisciplinary Context

Andrew N. Garman, PsyD, MS

LEARNING OBJECTIVES

After completing this chapter, the reader will be able to:

1. Describe similarities and differences in the motivational patterns associated with the selection of career paths in major health professions.
2. Characterize leadership challenges associated with working in an interdisciplinary context.
3. Apply the concepts of competencies and competency models to leadership development in health care.
4. Identify approaches to leadership development that are well-suited to interdisciplinary work.

KEY TERMS

Career choice theory
Competencies

Competency modeling
Competency models
Developmental assignments
Mentoring
Multisource feedback

INTRODUCTION

The Institute of Medicine's (IOM) widely publicized report, *To Err is Human: Building a Safer Health System* (Kohn, Corrigan, & Donaldson, 2000), made a strong case for interdisciplinary approaches to addressing shortcomings in the U.S. healthcare system. In their follow-up report, *Crossing the Quality Chasm* (IOM, 2001), the Institute of Medicine drew attention to the critical role that organizational systems play in ensuring patient safety and patient care. Effective interdisciplinary collaboration, in particular, is linked to improved outcomes for patients (IOM, 2003; Pew Health Professions Commission, 1998). In "Keeping Patients Safe: Transforming the Work Environment of Nurses" (2004), the Institute recommended that healthcare organizations support interdisciplinary collaboration, such as interdisciplinary rounds and education so that the professions can 'work smarter' together.

Healthcare providers are among the best-trained professionals of any industry. But highly trained professionals cannot by themselves overcome the limitations of the health delivery systems in which they work. Indeed, the depth of inculcation in these professions can be both a help and a hindrance to effective patient care delivery. With specialized training comes a greater natural resistance to alternative methods and approaches, as well as greater difficulty communicating approaches to others who are not similarly trained. Bridging these gaps between disciplines is often a key role that healthcare leaders play for their organization.

The move from a direct service role to a leadership role poses particular challenges for many healthcare professionals as well as for health administrators. This chapter focuses on the unique challenges that the interdisciplinary work of a leader can pose as well as the ways in which these challenges may be addressed through a proactive approach to leadership development. We begin with an overview of the interdisciplinary context, considering each of the major healthcare professional groups—physicians, nurses, and administrators—through the lens of career choice, professional preparation, and reward structures.

THE INTERPERSONAL CONTEXT OF INTERDISCIPLINARY WORK

Career choice theory (Ginzberg, Ginzberg, Axelrod, & Herma, 1951; Holland, 1996) suggests that individuals differ according to the kinds of core interests they have, and that these interests tend to drive their choice of careers. Research suggests that healthcare career choice also follows this pattern; individuals' selection of a specific healthcare profession to pursue is strongly affected by who that person is and the goals he or she seeks. Once the career path is chosen, the student may spend 10 or more years receiving formal education and close supervision from mentors within the profession, who include others who have chosen the same career path and those who share a similar profile of core interests. This long sequestration further affects how professionals come to view themselves, their professions, and the other professions with which they interact. It also affects how they relate to others in their profession and outside their profession. (Hojat et al., 1997). A summary of these influences is provided in Table 2-1.

Table 2-1. Defining Principles of Major Health Disciplines

	Physicians	Nurses	Health Administrators
Defining roles	Diagnosis and clinical care delivery	Patient care and advocacy	Organizational financial health
Career choice: primary pattern	Investigative	Social	Enterprising
Professional education: Competition and attrition	Highly competitive entry; very low attrition rate	Medium to low competitive entry; high attrition rate	Medium competitive entry; medium attrition rate
Educational preparation: duration	Uniformly long	Short, medium, long	Medium
Basis for reward: material	Procedure volume	Time	Support of organizational goals
Social	Clinical competence	Service to patients and coworkers	Prestige of position; influence

Source: Adapted from Garman, Leach, & Spector, 2006.

PHYSICIANS

Physicians have been the historical providers of health care (Moller, 2002), and health services delivery today remains dominated by MDs. Studies of career choice suggest that *investigative* types (individuals with an orientation toward science and scientific discovery) tend to gravitate toward careers in medicine, and that *realistic* types (individuals with an affinity for practical, hands-on physical activity) gravitate toward surgery (Elam, 1994; Petrides & McManus, 2004). Both the investigative and realistic types tend to deemphasize the interpersonal aspects of work (Garman et al., 2006), suggesting the practitioners of medicine or surgery may have a blind spot when it comes to understanding the importance of interpersonal process in maintaining a high-performing workplace.

Admission to medical school is among the most competitive of all the health disciplines, and as such tends to emphasize excellence in academic pursuits, science in particular. These elements combine to yield a selection process that tends to favor adaptability to environmental cues for success as well as relentless achievement orientation. The practical education tends to emphasize individual contributions, creating a focus on the physician as an independent practitioner rather than a member of an interdisciplinary team. Competitive rather than cooperative behaviors tend to be reinforced. Any signs of incompetence tend to be forcefully punished, characteristics that have led medical schools to be described as possessing a "culture of abuse" (Kassebaum & Cutler, 1998).

Once they have completed their training, physicians tend to be rewarded based on their productivity, which may be roughly described as the volume of procedures they provide minus the costs of supporting those procedures. Within this structure, time eventually ends up being the principal limiting factor on earning potential. Productive use of physician time is a highly sensitive subject in the interdisciplinary context.

Physicians entering leadership roles often find themselves challenged in reconciling their former professional relationships among physician peers with their new responsibilities as administrative influencers and decision-makers. The transition also typically involves some loss of professional identity through decreases in clinical workload, academic activity, or both (e.g., Fairchild, Benjamin, Gifford, & Huot, 2004). Given the growing recognition of this challenge, healthcare organizations have been increasingly recognizing the need for, and value of, establishing physician leadership development programs within their organizations (Leslie et al., 2005; McAlearney, Fisher, Heiser, Robbins, & Kelleher, 2005).

NURSES

In contrast to physicians, the nursing profession promotes more of a natural systems orientation. Research on career choice suggests that *social* types (individuals oriented toward interpersonal relationships) tend to gravitate toward nursing careers. Although the nursing profession has a very strong and structured educational base, there is considerable heterogeneity within the profession in terms of levels of educational preparation and type of licensure.

Given the larger relative number of nurses in many healthcare settings and the more systems-focused nature of nursing work, many organizations have a more clearly defined career track for nurses than for physicians and other health professions. In general, career progression within nursing tends to follow one of two tracks: one based on clinical expertise, the other based on management expertise. The clinical track typically involves continued education at the master's or doctoral level, and the designation of Advanced Practice Nurse. The management track may involve additional education in management, although many nurses move into management roles without additional academic credentials.

Within nursing, leadership has been robustly linked to numerous organizational outcomes, including increased staff perceptions of work group cohesion, lower job stress, higher self-efficacy, higher job satisfaction, greater organizational commitment, and improved retention (Gilmartin & D'Aunno, 2007).

HEALTH CARE MANAGERS

The core focus of the healthcare management profession involves ensuring that the health delivery system within which they work remains financially viable, so that it may continue to provide care for its patients. Research on career choice suggests that *enterprising* types (individuals who are interested in controlling and dominating) tend to select this career path.

In contrast with other health professions, healthcare managers typically receive advanced training in leadership skills as part of their formal education. This education is beneficial in their transition from graduate school into their first leadership roles. However, like nurses and physicians, the advanced education that health administrators receive is typically delivered in a silo, alongside other health administration students. This relative isolation of health administration students creates an identity for the profession but also results in many students graduating without exposure to or understanding of the personalities and operative styles of individuals occupying other health professions. Leadership development programs that expose healthcare managers early in their careers to other leaders with diverse professional backgrounds can be particularly helpful in providing these perspectives.

LEADERSHIP COMPETENCY MODELS

Use of competencies in the modern sense of the word traces back to the work of psychologist David McClelland (1973), who was seeking an approach to measuring aptitude that was more closely tied to practical outcomes. A modern definition of competencies and several related concepts is provided below:

- *Competencies*: characteristics of employees with behavioral implications that are thought to be associated with highly successful performance of their job
- *Competency model*: an integrated framework of competencies that are thought to associated with successful performance of a given job
- *Core competencies*: a set of competencies that extend across positions within an organization (i.e., are not specific to a given job or job family) that are thought to be critical to the overall success of a given organization
- *Competency modeling*: a systematic process for identifying and articulating competencies at one or more levels (individual, team, job family, and/or organization)

It is also important to distinguish "competencies" from the similar-sounding term, "competence." The latter term, which is often applied to clinical roles, generally refers to the minimally acceptable performance criteria associated with a given task or role. Competencies, in contrast, are designed to relate to highly successful performance. In other words, a person can have development needs in one or more competencies and still be quite competent in their role.

In recent years, in response to high-profile calls for greater attention to leadership development in health care, a substantial number of competency models have been disseminated that apply to healthcare leadership. A summary of the characteristics of several more prominent models is provided in Table 2-2.

To illustrate the nature and level of depth of these models, a more detailed description of one of them, the Health Administration Leadership (HAL) model, follows.

Table 2-2. Recent Competency Models Developed for Health Care Leadership Roles

Source(s)	Target Population	Goals	How It Was Developed	Structure
Ross, Wentzel, and Mitlyng (2002)	General (students and health administrators at all levels)	Provide an in-depth treatment of competencies relevant to health administration	Author experience and review of prior models	24 competencies in 4 clusters
American College of Medical Practice Executives (ACMPE; 2003)	Medical group management professionals	Develop and disseminate resources to advance the development of the profession	Subject matter expert panel plus validation with incumbent sample	5 competency clusters
Association of University Programs in Health Administration (AUPHA; Hilberman, 2004)	Graduate students and early careerists	Support pedagogy enhancement in graduate health administration education	Review of related competency models and consensus of expert panel	35 competencies in 3 clusters
Garman, Tyler, and Darnall (2004)	Early-, mid-, and senior-level healthcare managers	Identify behavioral competencies that distinguish higher from lower performers	Content validation with subject-matter experts	26 competencies in 7 clusters

(continues)

Table 2-2. Recent Competency Models Developed for Health Care Leadership Roles (continued)

Source(s)	Target Population	Goals	How It Was Developed	Structure
National Center of Healthcare Leadership (NCHL; 2004)	General (healthcare management and related fields)	Develop a benchmark model of core competencies for the profession	Qualitative meta-analytic review of prior competency models (Calhoun et al., 2004); refinement based on practitioner input	26 competencies in 3 clusters
Healthcare Leadership Alliance (HLA; 2005a, 2005b)	General (healthcare management at all levels)	Develop and disseminate resources for core and specialty competencies in health administration across subdisciplines	Collaboration of five major health administration professional associations (ACHE, AONE, HFMA, HIMSS, MGMA/ ACMPE)	300 competencies in 5 clusters
Dye and Garman (2006)	Senior-level executives	Support self-development in areas that differentiate the highest performers from other strong performers	Experiences of senior executive search consultants	16 competencies in 4 clusters

Source: Adapted from Garman & Johnson, 2006.

The Health Administration Leadership Competency Model

Garman, Tyler, and Darnall (2004) developed a competency model specific to healthcare leadership roles with interdisciplinary effectiveness as an explicit component of its model. The model was developed via in-depth interviews with executive search consultants specializing in top-level positions within healthcare organizations. Results of the interviews were iteratively categorized with the assistance of a semiautomated content analysis application, and converged into 26 competencies within 7 broad domains. These domains and their interrelationships are depicted graphically in Figure 2-1.

The figure depicts the domains in terms of two dimensions and two support functions. The first dimension relates to the extent to which a competency focuses on planning and preparation versus doing (execution); the second axis is the extent to which the competency focuses on process vs. people.

I. Charting the course. This domain relates to the quadrant that intersects "Planning and preparation" with "Process." These are the activities a leader does that involve longer term plans affecting the system-as-a-whole. Competencies in this domain include: strategic vision, innovativeness, systems thinking, and flexibility and adaptability.

II. Inspiring commitment. The other quadrant in "Planning and preparation" addresses the "People" side of these plans, in particular, the persuading, inspiring, and general capacity-building necessary to get staff invested

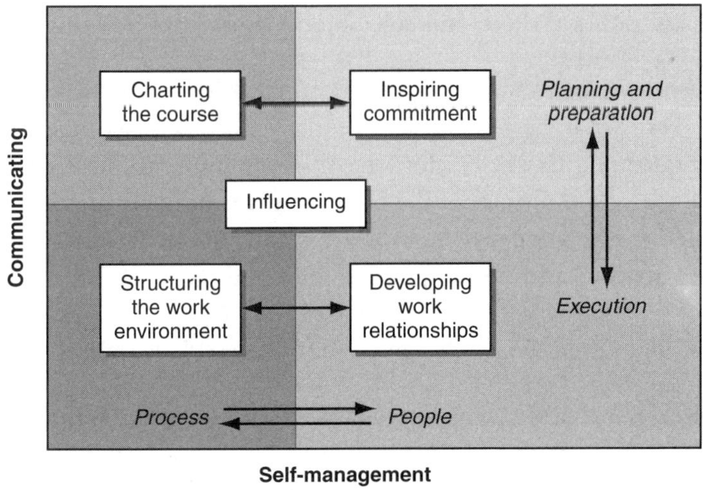

FIGURE 2-1. The Health Administration Leadership Competency Model
Source: Adapted from Garman, Tyler, & Darnell, 2004.

in the plans at an emotional level. The four competencies associated with this domain are: building trust, listening and feedback receiving, tenacity, and self-presentation.

III. Developing work relationships. This domain, located in the quadrant representing the intersection between "Execution" and "People," covers competencies related to bringing out the best from each employee through the work that they are engaged in. Competencies in this domain include: individual understanding, mentoring, and physician/clinician relations.

IV. Structuring the work environment. This domain, in the quadrant of the model representing the "Execution" and "Process" components, involves the leaders' activities related to arranging work processes and structures to optimize outcomes. The competencies in this domain are: work design a coordination, feedback giving and performance management, use of meetings, and decision-making.

V. Influencing. A leader's skill in successfully affecting the behavior and decisions of people over whom they have little or no formal authority will have a substantial impact on his or her effectiveness in all aspects of planning, execution, processes, and people. Thus, the influencing domain appears at the center of the quadrant, intersecting both axes and touching all dimensions. Competencies in this domain include: consensus-building, persuasiveness, political skills, and collaboration and team-building.

VI. Communicating. The communicating domain forms the model's left-hand border and represents a force that can drive the competencies in the four quadrants forward. Effectiveness in communications is thought to enhance the power of each of the other domains in the quadrant portion of the model. The competencies within this domain are: energizing, crafting messages, writing, and speaking.

VII. Self-management. The final competency domain forms the foundation on which the other domains in the model rest. Self-management describes a leader's abilities to recognize him- or herself as a finite resource, one with limitations that need to be worked with and around. The competencies within this domain are: managing limits, balance, and resilience and self-restraint.

Uses of Competency Models

Regardless of the leadership model an individual or organization adopts, competency models are, ultimately, not an end in and of themselves. They are only a means to an end, that end being performance improvement. For a competency model to lead to performance improvement, it must be meaningfully tied to leadership development practices.

LEADERSHIP DEVELOPMENT METHODS

Research on leadership development is very clear on two points. First is that the overwhelming majority of leadership competency development takes place on-the-job and within the context of work. Second, effective development of leadership competencies is greatly facilitated by the availability of high-quality performance feedback from subordinates, peers, superiors, and customers (Brutus, London, & Martineau, 1999; Hazucha, Hezlett, & Schneider, 1993; Walker & Smither, 1999). Combined, these findings suggest that the most effective leadership development programs will combine elements of practice along with opportunities for high-quality feedback on that practice. Research on leadership development methods tends to support this conclusion as it relates to healthcare professionals (e.g. McKenna, Gartland, & Pugno, 2004). Within that broad framework, a number of combinations of leadership development activities are possible. Healthcare organizations employ a variety of strategies for developing leadership skills depending on the local needs, preferences, and resources. According to recent research (Garman & Tyler, 2004; Garman & Tyler, 2006), the most commonly employed methods in healthcare organizations include: developmental assignments, mentoring, and 360-degree feedback.

Developmental Assignments

Developmental assignments are special projects and/or responsibilities that are assigned to leaders in order to help them gain experience or develop specific competencies. This is one of the most common methods for developing leaders, and even classroom-based leadership programs frequently will require developmental assignments as homework (e.g., Wakefield, Kienzle, Howell, & Kelch, 2005). In this way, developmental assignments can become the practice context in which leadership competencies are tempered by the "real-world" considerations that cannot be reasonably addressed within the artificial context of a classroom or workshop setting.

Developmental assignments are popular, but there has been little research to guide their selection and structure for maximum learning impact. A noteworthy exception is the work of McCauley and colleagues (1994), who developed a Job Challenge Profile by surveying hundreds of leaders from a variety of industries about the experiences that most influenced their own development. Their research identified five types of developmental assignments that were particularly powerful:

1. **Job transitions.** Assignments that required a leader to take an entirely new position, particularly if that new position involved new and unfamiliar responsibilities, or if the leader thought there was a substantial need to quickly establish credibility and "prove" her- or himself in this new role.
2. **Creating change.** Any assignments involving a substantial need for change might include taking the organization in a new direction, "inheriting" difficult conditions such as poorly structured departments or difficult employees, substantial reductions in resources, or challenges that their new employees were not initially well-trained or equipped to tackle.
3. **Higher-profile responsibilities.** These might include projects that had particularly high visibility within the organization and/or regular attention from senior leadership, ones with significant increases in job scope with subsequently high amount of time and energy demanded of them, or projects involving considerable scrutiny from outside groups or stakeholders.
4. **Influence-intensive roles.** These include developmental assignments in which the leader needed to involve a large number of participants and/or high-powered participants over whom they had no formal authority, and few 'bargaining chips' to use.
5. **Substantial structural and managerial obstacles.** Examples of developmental assignments with structural obstacles included projects with considerable resource shortages, or a lack of senior leader sponsorship and/or general organizational support. Developmental assignments with managerial obstacles involved leaders working for a superior whose style was either not a good match for their own, who was limited in managerial skills, or who was openly antagonistic.

Mentoring

Mentoring, broadly defined, includes any regularly occurring activity involving one-on-one meetings in which the leader's development is the principal focus of the dialogue. Defined in this way, mentoring could take place between a leader and his or her superior. Alternatively, it could occur between a leader and another person in the organization, typically a higher-level leader who is not part of the same chain-of-command.

Early research suggested that many high-achieving leaders reported benefiting from seeking out mentors early in their careers. These positive results led a number of organizations to implement formal mentoring programs, in which they attempted to proactively provide leaders with access to individuals who could serve as their mentors. Although both formal mentoring programs and informal mentoring have been found to have significant positive effects on career attainment, the informal approach appears to be significantly more powerful (Underhill, 2005), perhaps because it differentiates leaders who take the initiative to promote their own professional development from those who do not.

Multisource ("360-Degree") Feedback

Multisource ("360-degree") feedback involves the collection of survey data about an identified leader from various key individuals in that leader's domain of work: peers, subordinates, and sometimes superiors and clients. The surveys are usually distributed and collected by a neutral third party—a human resource staff member, external consultant, or secure Internet Web application—which then anonymizes and analyzes the data before delivering the formatted results to the leader. This aggregation and anonymization process helps ensure that survey respondents maintain their confidentiality, an important feature for diminishing fear of political repercussions from honest input.

The 360-degree feedback process can be developmental or it can be appraisal-based. A developmental 360 is used solely for performance improvement processes; typically the report of results and feedback is made available only to the leader to promote self-development. An appraisal-based 360, in contrast, is tied in some way to the formal performance appraisal process. Generally speaking, appraisal-based 360s provide less accurate and useful feedback because they quickly become part of the same political process that influences many performance appraisals. For this reason, many practitioners recommend that 360-degree feedback be used primarily for development rather than appraisal purposes.

The Health Administration Leadership competency model, described earlier in this chapter, has an associated 360-degree feedback item bank, which is provided in Table 2-3. To complete a feedback survey, the respondant would be asked to consider how effectively he or she thought

Table 2-3. 360-Degree Feedback Items Associated with the Health Administration Leadership Competency Model

I. Charting the course

- **Strategic vision**
  - Demonstrates a solid feel for the organization's purpose
  - Keeps track of important changes in the external environment as they may affect the organization
  - Effectively visualizes the organization's future based on organization and environmental knowledge
  - Creates a clear, appealing vision to which all can subscribe
  - Successfully aligns employees with that vision
- **Innovativeness**
  - Brings creative ideas to the table
  - Positively challenges others' ways of thinking
  - Explores uncharted options
  - Thinks "outside the box"
  - Identifies, explores, and utilizes all opportunities
- **Systems thinking**
  - Anticipates the ways changes in one department may affect other departments
  - Integrates all departments into planning and the "big picture"
  - Fosters relationships across departments that overcome "silo-ing"
- **Flexibility and adaptability**
  - Shows openness to new ideas and courses of action
  - Is willing to change positions
  - Is skillful and creative in problem-solving

II. Inspiring commitment

- **Building trust**
  - Communicates truthfully about all things including him- or herself
  - Follows through on promises and decisions
  - "Walks the talk"
  - Handles sensitive information appropriately and effectively

(continues)

Table 2-3. 360-Degree Feedback Items Associated with the Health Administration Leadership Competency Model (continued)

- **Listening and feedback receiving**
  - Knows when to listen and when to speak
  - Actively listens to others
  - Shows interest in others' opinions
  - Shows openness and an ability to "hear" criticisms
  - Listens without interrupting
- **Tenacity**
  - Shows courage in his or her convictions
  - Sticks to his or her guns when faced with push-back
- **Self-presentation**
  - Presents his or herself in a manner that puts others at ease
  - Shows professional stature
  - Dresses appropriately according to the environment and company
  - Acts as a host in all situations
  - Prepares well for all interactions
  - Relates well to others regardless of their position

III. Developing work relationships

- **Individual understanding**
  - Understands each employee and relating to each on a personal level
  - Understands what motivates each employee and acts accordingly to help the employee attain professional goals
- **Mentoring**
  - Acts as a role model for employees
  - Empowers others
  - Nurtures employees so they are equipped to achieve goals
  - Teaches others important lessons in an unassuming manner
- **Physician and clinician relations**
  - Views clinicians as partners rather than employees
  - Understands clinicians' professional roles and objectives
  - Demonstrates sensitivity to clinicians' needs
  - Shows mutual respect and tolerance toward clinicians' needs

IV. Structuring the work environment

- **Work design and coordination**
  - Delegates effectively (giving employees work without micromanaging)
  - Sets up reporting structures so that she or he has the right information at the right times
  - Multitasks effectively (i.e., can pursue multiple agendas at the same time)

(continues)

Table 2-3. 360-Degree Feedback Items Associated with the Health Administration Leadership Competency Model (continued)

- Recruits, retains, and counsels management toward effectiveness in their positions
- Sets clear and measurable objectives

- **Feedback giving and performance management**
  - Communicates clear and consistent messages about expected results
  - Assesses management performance clearly and credibly, and communicates these assessments routinely
  - Addresses performance problems in a timely and appropriate manner
- **Use of meetings**
  - Sets clear goals for meetings and then achieves them
  - Ensures that the meeting time is well-spent
  - Balances time pressure against the need for appropriate input from participants
- **Decision making**
  - Tries to obtain all important information before making a decision
  - Able to make decisions if necessary without having all information
  - Knows when to make a decision and when to wait
  - Able to make tough decisions without hesitating
  - Understands when the organization is and is not ready for change

V. Influencing

- **Consensus-building**
  - Understands all parties' agendas and uses that understanding to generate compromises
- **Persuasiveness**
  - Influences others to get onboard with organizational goals
  - Facilitates acceptance of changes
  - Creates and facilitates change in ways that minimize perceived threat
- **Political skills**
  - Demonstrates political savvy and good political instincts
  - Knows when to be proactive and when to "lay low" in respect to different issues and leaders
- **Collaboration and team-building**
  - Creates coalitions among employees around broader goals
  - Moves people toward team goals
  - Brings groups to consensus on team goals that satisfy everyone

(continues)

Table 2-3. 360-Degree Feedback Items Associated with the Health Administration Leadership Competency Model (continued)

VI. Communicating

- **Energizing**
  - Communicates and acts in ways that energizes others
  - Gets people energized and excited about their work
  - "Rallies the troops"
- **Crafting messages**
  - Creates messages and style according to the specific audience at hand
  - Delivers clear, concise, articulate messages
- **Writing**
  - Uses correct grammar and spelling in written communications
  - Writes messages that are clear and coherent
  - Pays attention to detail
- **Speaking**
  - Demonstrates well-developed podium skills
  - Speaks clearly, avoiding mixed messages

VII. Self-management

- **Managing limits**
  - Shows awareness of limits in knowledge and abilities
  - Seeks input from others with those strengths
  - Relies on others for information and support in areas of weakness
  - Shows awareness of limits in personal resources (i.e., time, focus, energy)
- **Balance**
  - Pursues interests outside of the organization
  - Balances work and family life effectively
  - Coordinates work and personal life to prevent one from undermining the other
- **Resilience and self-restraint**
  - Shows respect for ideas and opinions despite personal disagreement with them
  - Addresses concerns in positive and constructive ways
  - Keeps an even temper when frustrated

VIII. Open-ended questions

- Please provide at least one example to help clarify the feedback you are providing: (This question appears at the end of each competency.)
- In what way or ways has this person shown themselves to be particularly effective in your work with them?
- If this person could improve in one area, which one would make the biggest difference in their overall effectiveness?

that a given leader demonstrated each of the associated behaviors, using a provided rating scale. Respondents are also typically asked to comment on their judgments, using examples or other types of descriptions. Participants in 360-degree feedback programs often describe these open-ended responses as the most valuable part of the process, because they tend to contain much more specific ideas and advice on how to improve in a given area or areas.

Multiple Methods

Prior research suggests that multimethod approaches are more effective than single-method approaches (Garman & Tyler, 2004; Garman & Tyler, 2006). The combinations of methods that appear to be the most powerful involve some combination of a work experience component (developmental assignments or other projects) with a targeted source for feedback on development (e.g., mentoring, 360-degree feedback, or other assessment method).

CONCLUSION

Effective leadership has demonstrated a clear and consistent positive relationship to many outcomes of critical interest to healthcare organizations. It is also an activity that inherently involves trading short-term costs for long-term payoffs. Leadership development activities can be difficult to get going, and to maintain once they are in place. But, as the trends for increased quality, safety, transparency, and consumer-driven health care continue, the need for continuous improvement in leadership competencies will likely continue to gain increased support. Additionally, collaboration among organizations to identify the best and most-efficient practices, coupled with sharing and utilizing the most effective leadership development programs, should result in improved outcomes and quality of care for healthcare organizations and their clients.

DISCUSSION QUESTIONS

1. Research suggests that the private sector is far more involved in leadership development activities than most healthcare organizations. What kinds of barriers do you think may prevent healthcare organizations from adopting more of these practices?

2. One approach to bridging interprofessional gaps is to encourage clinicians to pursue administrative (MHA or MBA) degrees. What advantages and disadvantages do you see in this approach?
3. Healthcare professions are increasingly challenging one another's "exclusive rights" to provide services of various kinds, which may influence which professions provide what kinds of care in the future. Given the descriptions of the nursing and medicine professions above, what might be the effects of the nursing profession becoming more dominant in health services delivery? Of the medical profession becoming more dominant?

REFERENCES

American College of Medical Practice Executives (2003). The ACMPE® Guide to the Body of Knowledge for Medical Practice Management. Retrieved November 4, 2008, from http://www.mgma.com/workarea/showcontent.aspx?id=22924

Brutus, S., London, M., & Martineau, J. (1999). The impact of 360-degree feedback on planning for career development. *Personnel Psychology, 18*, 676–693.

Calhoun, J. G., Vincent, E. T., Baker, G. R., Butler, P. W., Sinioris, M. E., and Chen, S. L. (2004, Fall). Competency identification and modeling in healthcare leadership. *Journal of Health Administration Education*, 419–440.

Dye, C. & Garman, A. N. (in press). *Exceptional Leadership: 16 Critical Competencies for Healthcare Executives.*

Elam, C. (1994). Application of Holland's theory of vocational personalities and work environments to medical student specialty selection. *Journal of Career Development, 21*, 37–48.

Fairchild, D. G., Benjamin, E. M., Gifford, D. R., & Huot, S. J. (2004). Physician leadership: Enhancing the career development of academic physician administrators and leaders. *Academic Medicine, 79*, 214–218.

Garman, A. N. & Johnson, M. (2006). Leadership competencies: An introduction. *Journal of Healthcare Management, 51*, 13–17.

Garman, A. N., Leach, D. L., & Spector, N. S. (2006). Worldviews in collision: Conflict and collaboration across professional lines. *Journal of Organizational Behavior, 27*, 829–849.

Garman, A. N., & Tyler, J. L. (2004). "CEO succession planning in freestanding U.S. hospitals: Final report." White paper, American College of Healthcare Executives (ACHE). Retrieved July 1, 2008, from the ACHE Web site, http://www.ache.org/pubs/research/succession_planning.pdf

Garman, A. N., & Tyler, J. L. (2006). "CEO succession planning practices and outcomes in U.S. hospital systems: Final report." White paper, American College of Healthcare Executives (ACHE). Retrieved July 1, 2008 from the ACHE Web site, http://www.ache.org/pubs/research/succession_planning.pdf

Garman, A. N., Tyler, J. L., & Darnall, J. S. (2004). Development and validation of a 360-degree feedback instrument for healthcare administrators. *Journal of Healthcare Management, 49(5)*, 307–322.

Gilmartin, M. J. & D'Aunno, T. A. (2007). Leadership research in healthcare. *The Academy of Management Annals, 1:1*, 387–438.

Ginzberg, E., Ginzberg, S. W., Axelrod, S., Herma, J. L. (1951). *Occupational choice: An approach to a general theory*. New York: Columbia University Press.

Hazucha, J. F., Hezlett, S. A., & Schneider, R. J. (1993). The impact of 360-degree feedback on management skills development. *Human Resource Management, 32*, 325–351.

Healthcare Leadership Alliance. (2005a). HLA competency directory. Retrieved November 4, 2008, from http://www.healthcareleadershipalliance.org/directory.htm

Healthcare Leadership Alliance (2005b). HLA competency directory user's guide. Retrieved November 4, 2008, from http://www.healthcareleadershipalliance.org/HLA_Competency_Directory_Guide.pdf

Hilberman, D. (2004). AUPHA-ACHE pedagogy enhancement project on leadership for early careerists. Presentation at the AUPHA/ACHE Leaders' Conference, San Francisco, CA. Retrieved December 13, 2005, from http://www.aupha/org/pdf/hilberman.pdf

Hojat, M., Fields, S. K., Rattner, S. L., Griffiths, M., Cohen, M. J. M., & Plumb, J. D. (1997). Attitudes toward physician-nurse alliance: Comparisons of medical and nursing students. *Academic Medicine, 72(Suppl)*, S1–S3.

Holland, J. (1996). Exploring careers with a typology: What we have learned and some new directions. *American Psychologist, 51*, 397–406.

Institute of Medicine (2001). *Crossing the quality chasm: A new health system for the 21st century*. Washington, DC: National Academies Press.

Institute of Medicine (2004). *Keeping patients safe: Transforming the work environment of nurses*. Washington, DC: National Academies Press.

Institute of Medicine (2003). *Health professions education: A bridge to quality*. Washington, DC: National Academies Press.

Kassebaum, D. G., & Cutler, E. R. (1998). On the culture of student abuse in medical school. *Academic Medicine, 73*, 1149–1158.

Kohn, L. T., Corrigan, J. M., & Donaldson, M. S. (Eds.) (2000). *To err is human: Building a safer health system*. Washington, DC: National Academies Press.

Leslie, L. K., Miotto, M. B., Liu, G. C., Ziemnik, S., Cabrera, A. G., Calma, S., Huang, C., & Slaw, K. (2005). Training young pediatricians as leaders for the 21st century. *Pediatrics, 115*, 65–773.

McAlearney, A. S., Fisher, D., Heiser, K., Robbins, D., & Kelleher, K. (2005). Developing effective physician leaders: Changing cultures and transforming organizations. *Hospital Topics, 83(2)*, 11–18.

McCauley, C. D., Ruderman, M. N., Ohlott, P. J., & Morrow, J. E. (1994). Assessing the developmental components of managerial jobs. *Journal of Applied Psychology, 79*, 544–560.

McClelland, D. G. (1973). Testing for competence rather than 'intelligence.' *American Psychologist, 28*, 1–14.

McKenna, M. K., Gartland, M. P., & Pugno, P. A. (2004). Development of physician leadership competencies: perceptions of physician leaders, physician educators and medical students. *Journal of Health Administration Education, 21(3)*, 343–354.

Moller, M. T. (2002). *Directory of American Medical Education: 2002–2003*. Washington, DC: American Association of Medical Colleges.

NCHL (2004). Health Leadership Competency Model, version 2.0. Retrieved November 4, 2008, from http://www.nchl.org/ns/documents/CompetencyModel-short.pdf

Petrides, K. V., & McManus, I. C. (2004). Mapping medical careers: Questionnaire assessment of career preferences in medical school applicants and final-year students. *BMC Medical Education, 4(1)*, 18.

Pew Health Professions Commission (1998, December). Recreating health professional practice for a new century. *The Fourth Report of the Pew Health Professions Commission*. San Francisco, CA: Pew Health Professions Commission.

Ross, A., Wenzel, F. J., and Mitlyng, J. W. (2002). *Leadership for the future: Core competencies in healthcare*. Chicago, IL: Health Administration Press.

Underhill, C. M. (2005). The effectiveness of mentoring programs in corporate settings: A meta-analytical review of the literature. *Journal of Vocational Behavior, 68*, 292–307.

Wakefield, D. S., Kienzle, M. G., Howell, R. E., & Kelch, R. P. (2005). Building an institutional leadership development program: The University of Iowa Hospital and Clinics. In D. E. Detmer & E. B. Steen (Eds.), *The academic health center: Leadership and performance*. London: Cambridge University Press.

Walker, A. G., & Smither, J. W. (1999). A five-year study of upward feedback: What managers do with their results matters. *Personnel Psychology, 52*, 393–423.

CHAPTER 3

Fostering Interdisciplinary Collaboration in Health Care Organizations

Marsha Chan, PharmD, MBA, FACHE; Louis G. Rubino, PhD, FACHE

LEARNING OBJECTIVES

After completing this chapter, the reader will be able to:

1. Relate and describe current research and evidence supporting the benefit of collaboration across organizations in optimizing overall performance and promoting quality improvement.
2. Demonstrate an understanding of the benefits of organization-wide collaboration to achieve goals that are dependent upon multiple disciplines and functions.
3. Define and distinguish the essential components in developing and maintaining effective cross-functional collaboration.
4. List and describe processes to identify key stakeholders and define their role in leading, fostering, and sustaining a collaborative culture.

5. List and describe strategies to eliminate the challenges and barriers to creating a culture of collaboration.
6. Describe examples of successful organization-wide collaboration initiatives.

KEY TERMS

Evidence-based
Cross-functional
Process change
Continuum of care
Transparency
Process indicator(s) versus clinical indicator(s)
Performance improvement

INTRODUCTION

Collaboration has been demonstrated to be an effective tool in health care (Yeager, 2005; Cashman, Reidy, Cody, & Lemay, 2004). Collaboration and communication are identified as one of the 10 rules for redesign in the Institute of Medicine's (IOM) report, *Crossing the Quality Chasm* (IOM, 2001). Many healthcare professionals, however, have been trained to work only within the silos of their field and not across professional boundaries. Physicians, for example, have traditionally been mentored to practice as autonomous, independent practitioners (Kilo, 1999). But, research shows that high-quality care often requires the collaborative management of patients by a team that includes, for example, nurses, pharmacists, primary care and specialty physician consultants, laboratory technologists, respiratory therapists, and others. Effective communication and collaboration among interdependent professionals facilitates the achievement of the best outcomes for patients (Nembhard, 2007).

Modern healthcare delivery requires a complex organizational system, relying upon the coordination and integration of multiple services that are provided by a variety of caregivers, each with their own area of expertise and focus. The collaborative "team" approach is critical to successfully addressing the challenges of advancements in medicine and technology, limited resources, and burgeoning demand for services (Berry, 2004). Within any healthcare organization, this need for interdisciplinary collaboration occurs not only regarding the care of individual patients but also in support of system-wide processes and operations. Collaboration plays an important role both within single units and multiple departments, among professionals in a breadth of clinical and administrative fields.

ORGANIZATION-WIDE INTERDISCIPLINARY COLLABORATION

With the growing demand for accountability, hospitals are expected to verify the quality of care and services they provide. Successful survival in a challenging and competitive environment demands that hospital performance demonstrates the highest possible standard of care without sacrificing cost-efficiency. Interdisciplinary collaboration enhances the likelihood that high standards of care can be effectively achieved, even in large and complex organizations. The benefits of collaboration through healthcare teams for individual patients have been demonstrated and discussed above. But, healthcare outcomes are now being assessed on a larger scale, hospital-by-hospital, system by system. Collaboration involving the broader community of an entire organization and its patterns of function and operation is necessary for successful achievement of system-wide benchmarks and goals (Kilo, 1998; Kilo, Kabcenell, & Berwick, 1998).

Healthcare organizations striving to provide complex, high-quality, cost-efficient services need to incorporate or enhance collaborative processes in operational and clinical functions intra- and interdepartmentally. These collaborations, small- and large-scale, should include and be facilitated by stakeholders that represent the disciplines involved in providing the function or system of care.

DIFFERENTIATING SMALL VERSUS ORGANIZATION-WIDE COLLABORATIVE EFFORTS

Organization-wide collaboration is typically required in order to achieve large scale process operational or clinical quality improvement. Collaborative initiatives can be implemented within a small unit or department, or for an entire organization. There are identifiable differences in collaboration specifics depending on the scale of the system selected (see Table 3-1). An intradepartmental effort typically involves one discipline, is less complex, and has fewer variables. An organization-wide effort involves multiple disciplines, is more complex, and has more variables. Additionally, organization-wide collaborations are more identifiable and visible to an external audience. In general, these types of initiatives require more time, resources, and dedicated effort, yet if successful, they reap great benefits for the organization. In fact, collaborative efforts have been proven to accelerate and spread improvement (Institute for Healthcare Improvement [IHI], 2008a).

Table 3-1. Small-Versus Large-Scale Collaborative Efforts

	Small: Unit or Department Based	**Large: Organization-Wide**
Project example	Reduce the turnaround time for radiology reports to < 3 hours	100% appropriate care for inpatients diagnosed with congestive heart failure
Number of metrics	One	Multiple (In this example, there are four process measures)
Driver	Physician satisfaction Department performance metric	Strategic goal CMS, Joint Commission
Process(es)	Intradepartmental process	Multiple Cross-functional, interdependent processes
Variables (potential for variation)	Few	Many (individual MD practices, individual RN practices)
Stakeholders	Same or similar discipline	Multiple disciplines/ specialties (in this example: multiple nurses, pharmacists, physicians, echo technologists)
Visibility of outcome	Internal to department or organization	Internal and external visibility

ORGANIZATIONAL PERFORMANCE AS A DRIVER OF INTERDISCIPLINARY COLLABORATION

Large-scale interdisciplinary collaboration within a healthcare organization has a number of drivers. These include the organization's own performance improvement efforts that are directed by its strategic goals. The increased consumer demand for accountability and transparency of assessment data reflecting criteria such as quality of care, level of patient safety, and patient satisfaction, have added further motivation to demonstrate excellence.

Strategic Goals

Through the strategic planning process, healthcare organizations establish their strategic direction based upon a number of factors including their mission, vision, values, client and community needs assessment, and analysis of the organization's core competencies. The result is a balanced set of goals linked to performance in the areas of operational efficiency, quality, safety, customer service and finance (Institute for Healthcare Improvement (IHI). Execution of Strategic Improvement Initiatives To Produce System-Level Results. IHI Innovation Series, 2007). These strategic goals are typically large in scale. For example, a hospital may set goals such as "Deliver 100% Appropriate Care for Inpatients with Congestive Heart Failure" or "Patient Satisfaction in the 99th percentile." Clearly, goals of this magnitude are dependent upon the efforts of multiple disciplines and require collaboration beyond one or two departments of the hospital. Failure to achieve these complex goals, which are comprised of multiple steps and variables, can have a significant negative impact on an organization.

Transparency

In 2001, the Institute of Medicine identified the need for transparency as one of its 10 rules to redesign and improve care (IOM, 2001). Hospitals have adapted their practices to meet this recommendation. Examples include the employee consortium, the Leapfrog Group, which published hospital specific patient safety data on their Web site (Leapfrog, 2002). In 2005, the Hospital Quality Alliance unveiled their Hospital Compare Web site, which reported a set of standardized hospital quality measures. The Reporting Hospital Quality Data for Annual Payment Update (RHQDAPU) required hospitals to participate by submitting data on 21 clinical measures in 2007. In 2008, the collection and reporting of patient experience data (or HCAHPS) was launched on the Centers for Medicare & Medicaid Services (CMS) Hospital Compare Web site. There are many private rating companies that assess healthcare organization performance today, and insurers and some states have created report cards that can be used to evaluate and compare healthcare organizations.

With the increased demand for transparency, data are widely available reflecting an organization's performance in the management of patient experience data and clinical conditions such as acute myocardial infarction, congestive heart failure, and community acquired pneumonia. Each clinical measure set has between four to nine individual indicators (Joint Commission, 2008; CMS, 2008; IHI, 2008) that reflect processes of care across the continuum (i.e., in various care settings). A number of different disciplines and their representative stakeholders play essential roles in providing high quality care and thereby impacting collected data about an organization's performance.

FOSTERING A CULTURE OF INTERDISCIPLINARY COLLABORATION

Required Elements

A review of the literature identifies commonly cited attributes of successful interdisciplinary collaborative efforts, which cross over all industries and are summarized in Table 3-2. Consistently, across all sectors, an organization's culture of collaboration is driven by the philosophy and behavior of the top executives themselves. This modeling of collaborative behavior and the creation and promotion of a "gift culture" through mentoring and coaching have been identified as factors leading to successful collaborative teams in non-healthcare companies (Gratton & Erickson, 2007).

Parallel initiatives have been implemented in the healthcare industry. In 1995, The IHI designed the Breakthrough Series (BTS) as an approach to achieve large-scale improvements in clinical outcomes across multiple healthcare organizations. The BTS experience has identified factors that facilitate change and quality improvement through collaboration:

- Agreement on the aim
- Support and recognition by senior leadership
- Access to information (measures)

Table 3-2. Attributes of an Effective Interdisciplinary Collaborative Team

- Leadership support
- Constancy of purpose: shared vision and goal
- Effective communication
- Trust
- Mutual respect
- Shared accountability
- Individual ownership
- Expertise valued
- Focus on continuous improvement and learning
- Cohesiveness
- Stakeholder involvement

- Access to best practices
- Representation by key stakeholders
- Team members should be familiar with the process to be improved

At least three different types of expertise within the organization should be represented in a collaborative initiative (Baker, 1997). These include:

- System leadership (authority to institute change)
- Clinical technical expertise (guidance and know-how)
- Day-to-day leadership (details of system)

Additional studies focusing specific clinical investigations identified 11 requirements to fostering collaboration. In a report of 38 hospitals striving to reduce adverse drug reactions, the characteristics of successful collaboration included leadership (organizational and team level), a physician as part of the interdisciplinary team, stakeholder involvement, and selecting practical process changes (focus on process, not people; Leape et al., 2000). In another study, team cohesion and leadership (executive and clinical) were also identified in a review of collaborative methodology to improve congestive heart failure (Newton, Davidson, Halcomb, Denniss & Westgarth, 2006).

Barriers and Challenges

As in any worthwhile effort, there will be associated barriers and challenges (see Table 3-3) that may undermine a collaborative approach. Barriers

Table 3-3. Barriers and Challenges

- Lack of executive leadership support
- Poor team leadership
- Lack of shared vision and/or goal
- Resistance to change
- Resource constraints (i.e., time, equipment/supplies, money, people)
- Poor communication
- Lack of accountability
- Competitiveness
- Negative attitudes

include issues such as poor communication, a resistance to change, lack of accountability, negative attitudes, lack of coordination, competitiveness, lack of leadership (organization and team level), lack of a well-defined aim, and/or the lack of stakeholder involvement (Commonwealth Fund, 2008). In addition, the challenge of system inflexibility was identified as a characteristic of the bureaucracy of acute hospital environments (Newton, Davidson, Halcomb, & Denniss, 2007; Putland, Baum & MacDougall, 1997).

A number of individual and organizational issues can present as barriers and challenges to an interdisciplinary collaborative process. If not identified or addressed in a timely manner, these may stall and possibly derail successful collaboration. However, by recognizing and identifying the types of obstacles that may arise and hinder effective collaboration, leaders can implement specific and effective strategies to overcome challenges and support a positive outcome.

Strategies to Eliminate Barriers and Challenges

By identifying and understanding the types of barriers and challenges that organizations may face when initiating a given project, administrators, stakeholders, and team members can develop proactive strategies to avoid them and/or minimize their effect. The selection of skilled team members with the necessary proficiency and judgment is important to a project's success. Care should be taken at early stages of a collaborative process to identify the type of expertise required to solicit the participation of individuals with both the needed expertise and leadership and team-building capabilities among colleagues and peers. Both formal and informal leaders play an instrumental role in lending credibility to the project and in guiding project participants and others within the organization.

Ongoing executive leadership support and participation is another critical success factor. Thus, the appointment of an involved executive sponsor can demonstrate an ongoing commitment from the highest level of the organization. The executive sponsor also can be pivotal in removing potential barriers through resource allocation of staff, supplies, or funds.

The project team itself must begin with a thorough understanding of the goals of the project, that is, the problems to be addressed. If possible, a baseline assessment of the organization's current performance and identified benchmarks should be obtained. Comparative data reflecting best practice and community standards then can be used to establish the need for and scope of the improvement project. Evidence-based data from the literature can be powerful tools in defining the team's approach and in building the necessary support and consensus for change. Healthcare practitioners routinely use evidence-based findings in decision making and are likely to respond most positively to an evidence-based strategic approach.

The team's development of clearly understood goals and objectives is an important step in providing focus and direction for the team's subsequent efforts. The Institute for Healthcare Improvement advises that the aim statement(s) should be time-specific and measurable. Equally important is the allocation of people and resources to accomplish the aim. Finally, the identification of the populations that will be affected by the team's initiatives is important and consultation with the hospital's Institutional Review Board may be indicated (IHI, 2008a).

A written project plan with timelines can provide a framework for the team's approach and support effective communication and understanding of each member's responsibilities. Figure 3-1 depicts a sample project plan template.

To design and create an effective project, the team should ensure that end-users are consulted and that their input is considered in the project development. By including end-users in the design and planning phases, there is a greater likelihood of developing recommendations or guidelines that will be adopted and accepted by those responsible for day-to-day implementation. Once the project design is completed, roles and responsibilities for each process step and participant should be clearly delineated. This serves to promote clarity and accountability.

Project Title	
Description *Brief summary statement*	
Goal/AIM *Key outcome measure of success (what, by when, for whom)*	

Other metrics *Specific metric, the definition (numerator/ denominator if applicable), current baseline and target*	**Metric name**	**Definition (including Numerator/Denominator)**	**Baseline Performance (as of)**	**Target (Goal) Performance**

Unit/Dept(s) involved *List each Department* *In the design section, be sure each dept's role is clearly identified, including the individual or position responsibilities and the Dept Director's responsibility.*

Project leaders *Indicate team lead with an asterisk (*)*	*Name*	*Responsibilities related to this project*
Admin leader		
Nursing leader		
MD leader		
Quality lead		

Project design *(add more rows if necessary)*			
List key elements required	List specific TASK(S) to support the required element *Use separate row for each task. One key element may have multiple related Task(s) (Design note: consider risk of failure and design redundant processes to mitigate such risks)*	Identify individual responsible for each task *(by designation, i.e., operative MD, bedside RN)*	Additional detail

Implementation timeline *(include communication pieces)*			
Item	Responsible	Target date	Notes

References (literature, evidence-based)

FIGURE 3-1. Sample project plan

Source: St. Francis Medical Center, Lynwood, California. Used with permission.

The next phase of project development should include testing the designed guidelines or processes prior to full-scale implementation. This effort can help the team identify potential obstacles or issues that had not been effectively addressed, thus allowing for further refinement of the process prior to its official launch, and enhancing its chances of successful implementation.

Barriers and challenges to collaboration unfortunately can also impede and even derail a project. Organizations can minimize the impact of challenges and potentially eliminate them through careful and deliberate strategic planning on the front end of a collaborative project.

Ongoing communication among team members and stakeholders is critical throughout all stages of the project. Regularly timed communication to all stakeholders helps to ensure others are kept abreast of the project's progress and can play an integral role in providing internal feedback, effectively marketing the program (public relations), and preparing the organization for the upcoming implementation of the recommended changes.

Key Stakeholders

Research has shown that one of the characteristics of a successful collaborative process is the commitment and involvement of key stakeholders. In order to identify the stakeholders for a collaborative project, a review of the process(es) addressed and the participants involved is required. Through this analysis, units or disciplines involved in the process and the directors or managers of those units can be identified. As indicated previously, these parties should be included in the project team.

Other important stakeholders are those who can effectively serve as liaisons to groups to be impacted by the proposed changes. These may include a physician leader (MD champion) who can communicate with other key physicians and/or MD committees, a nursing leader, a unit administrator, and others.

Frontline staff members are also critical at all stages of the project planning. They can provide input that helps the planners to understand the strengths and weaknesses of existing processes and facilitate initial testing of the recommended changes (Nembhard et al., 2007). Patients and family members are stakeholders as well. Some organizations have instituted patient and family councils to allow and encourage input from their perspective regarding patient care and services (Dana-Farber, 2008). Depending upon the process under review, a business partner such as a vendor or contracted agency also may be a stakeholder and should be included on the team (see Table 3-4).

Strategies for Success

Though the organization's culture and executive level support for collaboration are important factors in developing successful collaborations, the effectiveness of the interdisciplinary team leader and the team itself will determine the level of collaborative success. Selection of the appropriate team leader and identification and inclusion of key stakeholders are critical factors for effective collaboration. A positive team dynamic is supported by establishing mutual trust and respect and a shared commitment to the team goals, maintaining an active desire to learn and improve, positively and effectively addressing conflicts, and containing negativity (Lindeke & Sieckert, 2005).

Table 3-4. Key Stakeholders

Stakeholder	Role
Executive leadership	Authority to institute change, allocate resources, breakdown barriers
Physician leader	Expertise, experience, ability to influence other physicians
Team leader	Provide direction, motivation, support team cohesiveness
Unit or department leaders and front-line staff	Those involved in some way with the process
Physician(s), nurses, ancillary staff	Those involved in some way with the process
Patients and families	Add their perspective as recipients of care and services
Business partners	As appropriate

CASE STUDIES

The following case studies are provided as examples of organization-wide interdisciplinary collaboration in a hospital setting. St. Francis Medical Center (SFMC) in Lynwood, California is a nonprofit, community-based, general acute care, 384-bed hospital sponsored by the Daughters of Charity, with over 2000 employees and 350 active medical staff. It hosts a high-volume emergency department and Level II Trauma Center, a high-volume obstetrical service (more than 7000 births/year), a neonatal intensive care unit (NICU), a 36-bed intensive care unit, a 40-bed inpatient psychiatric unit, a 30-bed skilled nursing center, 6 community based clinics, and comprehensive outpatient services.

Patient Safety

Since 2003, the Joint Commission has assessed healthcare organizations' compliance with the National Patient Safety Goals (NPSGs) with the aim of promoting specific improvements in patient safety (Joint Commission, 2008). Annually since 2005, the goals have been modified slightly to reflect additional requirements. The NPSGs for 2008 are depicted in Table 3-5.

The NPSGs have applicability across all patient care areas and disciplines. Evidence of noncompliance during an accreditation or unannounced survey will result in a Requirement for Improvement (RFI), which ultimately can negatively impact the organization's accreditation status if not effectively resolved.

In addressing each of the NPSGs at St. Francis, the Patient Safety Manager assessed SFMC's current policy and practices to determine its level of compliance and the need for policy revision. For those NPSGs requiring a change in policy, an interdisciplinary team of practitioners was formed. The composition of each team varied depending upon the specific NPSG being addressed. In addressing the communication of critical values (highly abnormal test results), NPSGs 2A and 2C, the team included department directors representing each area that potentially might report a critical value (laboratory, cardiology, respiratory, and imaging) as well as each area that might receive a critical value report (nursing directors, staff nurses, and physicians). The Patient Safety physician (champion) served as the liaison between the project team and other St. Francis physicians.

The team asked the medical staff departments and committees to reach agreement on those values that were "critical" and requiring immediate physician notification. The team then focused on process, including the manner in which the communication must occur, the appropriate time frame within which the communication must occur, and the manner

Table 3-5. National Patient Safety Goals, 2008

Goal #	Requirement
1	Improve the accuracy of patient identification
1A	Use at least two patient identifiers when providing care, treatment, or services
2	Improve the effectiveness of communication among caregivers
2A	For verbal or telephone orders or for telephonic reporting of critical test results, verify the complete order or test result by having the person receiving the information record and "read-back" the complete order or test result
2B	Standardize a list of abbreviations, acronyms, symbols, and dose designations that are not to be used throughout the organization
2C	Measure and assess, and if appropriate, take action to improve the timeliness of reporting, and the timeliness of receipt by the responsible licensed caregiver, of critical test results and values
2E	Implement a standardized approach to "hand off" communications, including an opportunity to ask and respond to questions
3	Improve the safety of using medications
3C	Identify and, at a minimum, annually review a list of look-alike/sound-alike drugs used by the organization, and take action to prevent errors involving the interchange of these drugs
3D	Label all medications, medication containers (e.g., syringes, medicine cups, basins), or other solutions on and off the sterile field
3E	Reduce the likelihood of patient harm associated with the use of anticoagulation therapy
7	Reduce the risk of healthcare-associated infections
7A	Comply with current World Health Organization (WHO) Hand Hygiene Guidelines or Centers for Disease Control and Prevention (CDC) hand hygiene guidelines
7B	Manage as sentinel events all identified cases of unanticipated deaths or major permanent loss of function associated with healthcare-associated infections

(continues)

Table 3-5. National Patient Safety Goals, 2008 (continued)

Goal #	Requirement
8	Accurately and completely reconcile medications across the continuum of care
8A	Establish a process for comparing the patient's current medications with those ordered for the patient while under the care of the organization
8B	A complete list of the patient's medications is communicated to the next provider of service when a patient is referred or transferred to another setting, service, practitioner, or level of care within or outside the organization. The complete list of medications is also provided to the patient on discharge from the facility.
9	Reduce the risk of patient harm resulting from falls
9B	Implement a fall reduction program including an evaluation of the effectiveness of the program
13	Encourage patients' active involvement in their own care as a patient safety strategy
13A	Define and communicate the means for patients and their families to report concerns about safety and encourage them to do so
15	The organization identifies safety risks inherent in its patient population
15A	The organization identifies patients at risk for suicide
16	Improve recognition and response to changes in a patient's condition
16B	The organization selects a suitable method that enables healthcare staff members to directly request additional assistance from a specially trained individual(s) when the patient's condition appears to be worsening

Source: © The Joint Commission, 2010. Reprinted with permission.

in which it must be documented. The team consulted with colleagues at other institutions and researched best practices. This analysis required the team members to look beyond their own immediate scope of responsibility and to gain understanding of the processes in other departments and institutions.

As might be expected, each discipline had its own opinions as to what should be considered the appropriate time frame for reporting a critical value to a nurse and physician. After reaching consensus, the team revised policies and documentation tools, identified staff and physician education needs, established the implementation timeline, and developed mechanisms to monitor organizational compliance.

The team's recommendations and the revised policies were then presented to the medical staff committees for approval. At this point, many physicians were hearing about the critical value reporting requirement for the first time and many challenged the required turnaround time for reporting; some believing the time should be longer, others believing it should be shorter. This feedback highlighted the importance and necessity of active communications from the committee or its representative liaisons with stakeholder groups.

In this case, the support of the Medical Executive Committee and other key physician leaders was secured after hearing from a patient safety expert at their medical staff leadership retreat. The speaker emphasized the necessity of a defined turnaround time for reporting critical values. Hearing this advice from a respected expert in the field was instrumental in garnering the medical staff leadership's support resulting in approval of the team's recommendations.

The next phase was implementation of the collaborative team recommendations. At the department level, process work flows for each of the reporting departments were redesigned and staff members were trained in the new procedures. The entire process from the planning stage to full implementation occurred over approximately six months.

This approach worked. It brought together individuals who typically work independently and encouraged them to address an identified issue collaboratively. Participation on the team allowed stakeholders to gain a better appreciation of the challenges faced in other disciplines and departments. For example, the physicians involved with the project gained a much better understanding of the workflow and steps involved to support critical value reporting. Team participants engaged in active learning by exploring effective approaches and best practices employed by other organizations. Physicians who were involved with the project then took on the role of spokespersons and mentors, helping to educate their peers about the NPSG and the rationale for the team's recommendations. It is worth noting that this general approach subsequently has been used for each of the NPSGs at St. Francis.

Patient Throughput

Many hospitals are challenged by patient throughput, defined as the flow of patients from the emergency department (or other point of admission) to discharge. Multiple factors impact each stage of the process and the literature is replete with the approaches organizations have taken to address this problem. Because there are so many variables and processes impacting throughput, SFMC has divided throughput into three separate components: throughput within the emergency department (ED) itself, ED to an inpatient bed, and inpatient stay to discharge.

This is another example of a challenge facing the entire medical center. Almost every department and discipline of the hospital is impacted by the inability to move patients through the system efficiently. Similarly, these same parties themselves have the potential, large or small, to impact patient throughput. Again, the scope and breadth of the challenge of improving patient throughput benefited from an interdisciplinary collaborative approach.

One main interdisciplinary oversight team was established along with several smaller subteams that focused on specific components of the throughput problem. The composition of the primary team included the SFMC Chief Operating Officer, the Chief Nursing Officer, the Vice President of Ancillary and Support Services, the Vice President of Quality Management, the ED Nursing Director, the ED Medical Director, and the directors for admitting, case management, and environmental services. When needed, the directors of finance, pharmacy, laboratory, and imaging, as well as staff ED nurses were at the table to help address specific challenges. It is important to note that this team included several executive representatives. The executive presence spoke to the importance of throughput to the organization, served to facilitate resource allocation, and helped keep the issue at the forefront of strategic planning efforts. As a result, there are several patient throughput goals and objectives included in the organization's strategic plan and bimonthly progress reports on throughput are presented to the Quality and Patient Safety Committee of the Board of Directors.

Due to this interdisciplinary team collaboration, progress was made to enhance and streamline many of the processes and functions within the ED. The focus of SFMC's quality improvement efforts regarding throughput has now shifted to the inpatient side, ensuring the patients' level of care and placement are appropriately matched and that a timely discharge occurs. To address this aspect of the issue, fewer ED representatives were needed on the collaborative team, and more physician leaders involved in inpatient care were recruited to garner more widespread hospital physician support.

Core Measure and CMS Clinical Indicator Set: Congestive Heart Failure

The final example provided will outline not only the interdisciplinary collaboration required to impact the management of congestive heart failure patients at SFMC, but also provide an example of the sharing of information with interdisciplinary teams of other hospitals in a multihospital collaborative.

Congestive heart failure (CHF) is the most prevalent medical condition for SFMC patients and is one of the first Joint Commission core measure sets selected by the organization in 2002. Initially, the organization simply collected and submitted its performance data to the Joint Commission. Attempts to improve performance were largely reliant upon communicating the results through the medical staff departments and educating physicians about the indicator definitions. As reflected in the organization's performance data, progress in achieving quality improvement benchmarks was slow.

A physician champion was identified, who assisted in developing strategies to improve one aspect of the Quality Improvement (QI) efforts, physician prescribing and documentation. However, rather than addressing the management of CHF as a system issue, the primary improvement focus at that time was on individual physician practices.

In October 2003, SFMC joined the Center for Medicare and Medicaid Services-Premier Hospital Quality Demonstration Project, a three year pay-for-performance demonstration project made available to those hospitals utilizing the Premier Clinical Informatics System. Participation in this project raised performance expectations by the SFMC Board of Directors and executive administration leading to the development and inclusion of specific performance goals for CHF in the organization's strategic plan. The organization now approached CHF management as a systems issue versus an individual practice matter.

An interdisciplinary team was formed that included the Medical Director for Cardiology, the Clinical Director for acute care services, and the Directors of Pharmacy, Quality, and Cardiology. The SMFC Performance Improvement Coordinator facilitated the meetings and data collection. The team regularly reviewed best practices posted to the demonstration project's Web site and participated in monthly conference calls with other hospitals across the country. The team designed and implemented SMFC processes and tools to support each of the four indicators (see Table 3-6). To minimize the risk of failure, redundancy was purposely built into the process. A concurrent review process was implemented to allow for real-time monitoring and to support immediate intervention and coaching of physicians and nurses if needed.

This project was further enhanced by SFMC's participation in the larger collaborative effort of the Institute for Healthcare Improvement's 5 Millions Lives Campaign in 2006 (Institute for Healthcare Improvement (2006). Protecting 5 Million Lives from harm. Retrieved November 2, 2008 from http://www.ihi.org/IHI/Programs/Campaign/Campaign.htm?TabId=1), which included data about the delivery of reliable, evidence-based CHF care. This multihospital collaborative further expanded the access to best practices and provided the organization with additional motivation to improve CHF management (see Figure 3-2).

Over the course of the demonstration project, SFMC's performance for each of the CHF process measures steadily improved, achieving 95–100% compliance after four years. This example dramatically demonstrates

Table 3-6. Core Measure and CMS Indicator Set for Congestive Heart Failure

	Ability to Impact the Measure				
Process Measure	**MD**	**RN**	**Pharmacist**	**Cardiology**	**Quality**
ACE inhibitor or ARB for left ventricular dysfunction	X	x	x		x
Left ventricular function assessment	X	x		X	x
Smoking cessation education provided	x	X			
Discharge instructions given (with 5 required elements)	X	X			

Symbols are: X = primary role; x = secondary role, ability to facilitate.
Source: St Francis Medical Center. Used with permission.

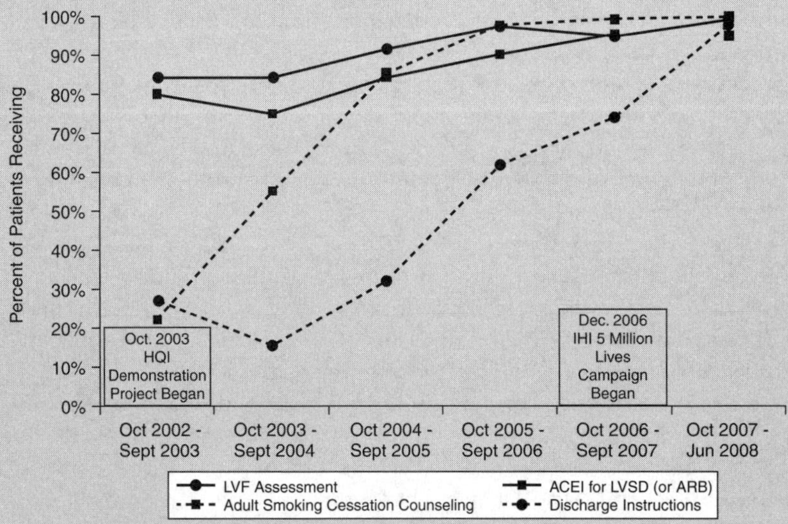

FIGURE 3-2. Congestive Heart Failure

Source: St. Francis Medical Center, Lynwood, California. Used with permission.

the benefit to SFMC's CHF care management by the use of an interdisciplinary collaborative process across the organization. Further benefits resulted from SFMC participation in two large multihospital collaboratives that provided greater access to best practices and served to add a competitive motivational boost to the local improvement effort.

CONCLUSION

Healthcare organizations today face increased scrutiny by patients, families, insurers (including the government), and competitors as well as the general public. With an increasing call for, and commitment to, accountability and transparency, an organization's accreditation survey results, clinical quality performance data, and patient satisfaction data have become public benchmarks that determine the effectiveness of quality of care and service. Today's competitive healthcare environment demands that healthcare organizations maximize the effectiveness of their services as demonstrated by assessment data.

Healthcare performance improvement efforts are evidence-based and employ quality improvement techniques common to production manufacturing. There is a greater focus on systems and processes rather than individual practice. These systems and processes are supported by a breadth of clinical and technical practitioners, many who are accustomed to working independently of one another. Yet, the complexity of modern healthcare delivery systems, combined with the demands for the highest quality of care, requires organization-wide interdisciplinary collaboration to maximize effectiveness. Interdisciplinary collaborative teams composed of those independent disciplines with a stake in the process, strong team leaders, and executive commitment are all essential to the success of any collaborative effort. Through these teams, organizations can instill and reinforce the need for effective communication, sharing knowledge, and continuous learning among stakeholders critical to the success of collaborative initiatives.

Growth and change are hallmarks of successful organizations, including healthcare organizations. Organization-wide interdisciplinary collaboration can promote large scale quality improvement and professional success for a healthcare organization, its constituents, and its clients.

DISCUSSION QUESTIONS

1. Why is it important to identify the key stakeholders for a collaborative initiative?
2. What are potential barriers to effective collaboration? What strategies can a team adopt to ensure these do not derail their efforts?
3. Is interdisciplinary collaboration more applicable to small-scale versus large-scale efforts? When is it critical to a successful outcome? When might it be less necessary?

REFERENCES

Baker, G. R. (1997). Collaborating for improvement: The Institute for Healthcare Improvement's Breakthrough series. *New Medicine, 1*, 5–8.

Berry, L. L. (2004). The collaborative organization: Leadership lessons from Mayo Clinic. *Organizational Dynamics, 33(3)*, 228–242.

Cashman, S., Reidy, P., Cody, K., & Lemay, C. (2004). Developing and measuring progress toward collaborative, integrated, interdisciplinary health care teams. *Journal of Interprofessional Care, 18(2)*, 183–196.

Centers for Medicare & Medicaid Services (CMS). (2008). Retrieved October 9 from http://www.hospitalcompare.hhs.gov

Commonwealth Fund. (© 2004–2008). *Section II—Building collaboration: The recruitment, retentions and recognition of partners.* Retrieved October 9, 2008 from http://www.commonwealthfund.org/General/General_show.htm?doc_id=381957

Dana-Farber Cancer Institute. (© 2001–2008). *Patient and family advisory council.* Retrieved October 9, 2008 from http://www.dana-farber.org/pat/support/adult-advisory/committees.asp

Gratton L., & Erickson T. J. (2007). Ways to build collaborative teams. *Harvard Business Review, 85*, 101–109.

HCAHPS: Patients' Perspectives of Care Survey (2008). Retrieved November 2, 2008 from http://www.cms.hhs.gov/HospitalQualityInits/30_HospitalHCAHPS.asp

Hospital Quality Alliance. (2008). Hospital Compare: a quality tool for adults, including people with Medicare. Retrieved October 9, 2008 from http://www.hospital compare.hhs.gov

Institute for Healthcare Improvement (IHI). (April 2008). *Collaboratives can accelerate and spread improvement.* Retrieved October 9, 2008 from http://www.ihi.org/IHI/Topics/Improvement/ImprovementMethods/ImprovementStories/FSCollaboratives CanAccelerateSpreadImprovement.htm

Institute for Healthcare Improvement (ISI). (N/A). Setting aims. Retrieved October 9, 2008 from http://www.ihi.org/IHI/Topics/Improvement/ImprovementMethods/HowToImprove/setting+aims.htm

Institute of Medicine (IOM). (2001). *Crossing the quality chasm: A new health system for the 21st century.* Washington, DC: National Academy Press; 322–335.

Joint Commission. Performance Measurement Initiatives. Retrieved November 3, 2008 from http://www.jointcommission.org/PerformanceMeasurement/Performance Measurement/

Joint Commission. National Patient Safety Goals. Retrieved November 3, 2008 from http://www.jointcommission.org/patientsafety/nationalpatientsafetygoals/Kilo, C. (1998). A framework for collaborative improvement: Lessons from the Institute for Healthcare Improvement's Breakthrough Series. *Quality Management in Healthcare, 6*, 1–13.

Kilo, C. (1999). Improving care through collaboration. *Pediatrics, 103*, 384–393.

Kilo, C.M., Kabcenell, A., & Berwick, D. M. (1998). Beyond survival: Toward continuous improvement in medical care. *New Horizons, 6*, 3–11.

Leape, L. L., Kabcenell, A. I., Gandhi, T. K., Carver, P., Nolan, T. W., & Berwick D. M. (2000). Reducing adverse drug events: Lessons from a Breakthrough Series Collaborative. *Journal on Quality Improvement, 26*, 321–331.

Leapfrog Group Press Release. (Nov. 14, 2002). 70 percent of all Americans can now get Leapfrog patient safety information for all hospitals in their area. Retrieved October 9 from http://www.leapfroggroup.org/media/file/Leapfrog-New_Region_Data_Release_11-14-02.pdf

Lindeke, L. L., & Sieckert, A. M. (2005). Nurse-physician workplace collaboration. *The Online Journal of Nursing*. Retrieved October 9 from http://198.65.150.241/OJIN/topic26/tpc26_4.htm

Nembhard, I. M., Tucker, A. L., Horbar, J. D., & Carpenter, J. H. (2007). Improving patient outcomes: The effects of staff participation and collaboration in healthcare delivery. *Harvard Business School Working Knowledge, No. 08-002.*

Newton, P. J., Davidson, P. M., Halcomb, E. J., & Denniss, A. R. (2007). Barriers and facilitators to the implementation of the collaborative method: reflections from a single site. *Quality and Safety in Health Care, 16*, 409–414.

Newton, P. J., Davidson, P. M., Halcomb, E. J., Denniss, A. R., & Westgarth F. (2006). An introduction to the collaborative methodology and its potential use for the management of heart failure. *Journal of Cardiovascular Nursing, 21*, 161–168.

Putland, C., Baum, F., & MacDougall, C. (1997). How can health bureaucracies consult effectively about their policies and practices? Some lessons from an Australian study. *Health Promotion International, 12*, 299–309.

Reporting Hospitals Quality Data for Annual Payment Update. (2007). *RHQDAPU program overview*. Retrieved October 9, 2008 from http://www.qualitynet.org/dcs

Yeager, S. (2005) Interdisciplinary collaboration: The heart and soul of health care. *Critical Care Nursing Clinics of North America, 17*, 143–148.

CHAPTER 4

Doctors Are From Mars; Patients Are From Venus

Vicki Rackner, MD, FACS

LEARNING OBJECTIVES

After completing this chapter, the reader will be able to:

1. Differentiate between the needs and expectations of a doctor and of a patient.
2. Understand the historical hierarchical doctor-patient relationship and its evolution towards a collaborative partnership between patient and doctor.
3. Compare the job description of a doctor versus a patient and define the role of each party in the collaboration.
4. Understand skills for achieving a common vision of care.
5. Understand the concept and role of the medical home.
6. Critique whether patient report cards are or are not helpful in ensuring high-quality health care.

KEY TERMS

Patient-centered care
Physician-centered curing
Medical home
Linear thinking
Zero-sum game

Munchausen syndrome
Health outcomes

INTRODUCTION

Two intimate partners have come together to serve a shared vision. But, instead, they keep running into the same conflicts. Each is frustrated that the other approaches a problem so differently. He wants to fix things; she wants to know that she is not alone facing the problem. He takes pride in her ability to solve problems; she gathers strength and courage in knowing they face the problem together. For him, revisiting a problem that does not have a solution is like nails on a chalkboard; even when the problem does not have a solution, she feels better when she can talk about how the problem impacts her life. While both of them want problems fixed, her highest priority is the feeling connected with his partner. He says, "Why doesn't she just get to the point?!" He says, "Why won't she just listen?"

While this could be a scene from a family counselor's office, I have just described a different partnership: the intimate relationship between doctor and patient when they come together to face health challenges.

The "professional" doctor–patient relationship is often as intimate as a committed personal relationship. The two parties can have wildly divergent points of view without even being aware of these critical differences. When people in a relationship make assumptions about the wants and needs of their partners, turmoil often ensues. The same holds true in the partnerships between doctors and patients.

Patients and physicians enter—and leave—the exam room with unrecognized differences in perspectives, expectations, and agendas. Physicians and patients may hold very different ideas about the destination to which medical care leads. Despite the sunny TV ads, few patients are excited about a drop in serum cholesterol, a number; their excitement comes from the hope that, by aiming for better health, they will see their grandchildren married or hike in the Grand Canyon or age in the homes they love. However, our current doctor-centered system of healthcare delivery leaves little room for recognition and acknowledgment of the patients' expectations and agenda.

Failure to understand our patients' perspectives contributes to troubling trends reported in both the medical and lay literature that negatively impact our patients' health. According to a recent *Consumer Reports* survey (Consumer Reports, 2008), patients almost unanimously said they "completely" or "mostly" followed their doctor's advice, but 59% of doctors said their patients often failed to adhere to the prescribed course of treatment. Growing numbers of patients express dissatisfaction with their medical care. Some turn away from their physicians and seek alternative health interventions. Others abandon treatment, or even turn against their physicians with legal charges.

In light of these differences in needs and expectations between doctors and patients, how can we create a system of healthcare delivery in which the patient—not the doctor—is the guest of honor whose needs are served? This is one of the great challenges before us. It's also a great opportunity for every party involved in health care to improve the quality of care delivered and provide a potential source of satisfaction and reward for all.

How are Doctors and Patients Different?

Imagine traveling to a different country where English is rarely spoken, the customs are dissimilar, and even the alphabet is even unfamiliar. Simple tasks such as finding a restroom or ordering a meal may become very challenging. Patients experience that same frustration when they enter the healthcare system. Healthcare professionals speak a language that's sort of like English, but is really a language unto its own. Additionally, every member of the healthcare team has a separate "job description," that is, a role and place in this alien medical culture, and few step out of their bounds to communicate in a familiar way or language. While health professionals walk the paths of illness every day, this world of medicine and health care is unfamiliar territory for most lay people.

You get the most out of travel when you're at your best, but unfortunately patients are usually at their worst. They're scared, confused, overwhelmed, and disoriented. Medication can further cloud their ability to think clearly. The patient is the party with the suffering; the doctor has the tools to alleviate the suffering. The patient needs entry through locked doors to medical services, and the healthcare professionals hold the keys. How can the patient effectively communicate his or her needs for treatment and relief when ill, injured, or frightened?

The result of these realities is that there is an imbalance of power between doctors and patients that reduces the effectiveness and the outcome of their collaborative interactions. Healthcare professionals are on their home turf, able to apply their judgment, skill, and experience to work through challenges; patients are tourists in this confusing, intimidating place. An effective collaboration should provide patients with a helpful map and tour guide and means to translate the foreign language of medicine, and encourage doctors to learn the "languages" of patients and to communicate in those languages.

What Is the Doctor's Job and What Is the Patient's Job?

Using an image of ballroom dancing lessons, patients and physicians can be thought of as being engaged in a dance around disease. The Latin roots suggest their roles. The word *patient* is derived from the Latin root *pati* meaning "one who suffers," while the word *doctor* comes from *docere*, meaning "to teach." Traditionally, doctors lead this dance and patients follow. Many patients are guided by the advice offered to the women by the dance instructor, "Your job is to follow, even if your partner is doing it wrong." I suggest a more collaborative dance routine: folk dancing and jazz dancing provide opportunities for each partner to express themselves in a positive and functional way.

Despite technologic advances, the most powerful medical intervention we have is still a trusting, caring relationship between a patient and a doctor. Patients get the best care when they and their doctor work well together as a team. Historically, the interactions between doctor and patient have been patriarchal, like those between a parent and a child. As patients and doctors, we're now evolving into an adult–adult collaboration, resulting in improved healthcare outcomes and increased patient adherence.

What Would a Job Description for an Ideal Doctor Look Like?

"Wanted: Caring professional with excellent communications skills, solid clinical judgment, and honed technical abilities whom I can proudly call 'My Doctor.' You collect key medical and personal information and put the puzzle pieces together in a way that makes sense. You recognize that I am the expert on my own body, and offer insights based on your knowledge and experience that guide me to choices that make most sense for me. When we don't see eye-to-eye, we respectfully agree to disagree. I trust you deeply. One day my life could be in your hands."

How About a Job Description of Your Ideal Doctor's Patient?

"I'm in the driver's seat in my journey to health. I recognize that all day-to-day lifestyle choices can lead in the direction of health or disease. I want to make consistent choices that lead to health. If I get sick, I collaborate with my doctor to restore my health."

Patients get the best, safest, and most cost-effective health care when they assume ultimate responsibility for their health. But it is wise for patients to let the doctor be the doctor, that is, to share his or her expertise and judgment and provide guidance and input for patients' decision-making processes. Good health care is not an end in itself; health care is a means to a healthy life best achieved in partnership with one's doctor.

How Important is the Patient's Perspective?

With so many concerns in the healthcare system screaming for attention, is sensitivity to the patient experience worthy of our attention, focus, and dedication, or is it just feel-good fluff? I would argue that understanding the patient's perspective is the very linchpin of healthcare transformation.

Doctors can be brilliant diagnosticians and skilled masters in therapeutic interventions. But without empathy and sensitivity to the patient's experience, the brilliant outcomes will not be forthcoming. The willingness of patients to tell their stories, to relate their symptoms, their fears, and the way the disease impacts their life influences the care they receive. Doctors can arrive at a diagnosis about 80% of the time just by listening to a patient's story. Conversely, patients who cannot overcome their fears of embarrassment or shame and open up to their doctor can end up harming themselves by not getting the care they need.

For example, as a physician, I had a patient who literally died of embarrassment. She thought that if the doctor needed to know about the blood in her stool, he would ask. She just wrote it off as "hemorrhoids." Had she told her doctor about her "embarrassing" symptom, the colon cancer that caused the blood would have been treatable. The delay in speaking up cost this patient her life.

Patients who cannot afford prescribed medications, who don't understand or believe the doctor's diagnosis, or who have intolerable side effects may not follow through with the doctor's outlined treatment plan. The result could be a negative outcome. Until the doctor and the patient come to a conceptual agreement, the verbal contract outlining the next steps will not be honored.

THE SUCCESSFUL APPOINTMENT: TWO PERSPECTIVES

From the Doctor's Side of the Bed

Doctors are groomed in the fine art of fixing patients' health problems. They are drilled in a linear thinking process that includes:

- Listening to the patient's story
- Gathering information from the physical exam and laboratory tests done
- Arriving at a diagnosis or at least identifying a few ways the puzzle pieces fit together
- Offering helpful or curative treatment
- Assessing progress toward elimination of symptoms

Doctors measure success through objective evidence and outcomes. If the patient is cured, then they have succeeded. The most satisfying interactions for many doctors are those in which there is a clear diagnosis, and a clear treatment that offers a cure. A patient with appendicitis, for example, offers a chance for excellent patient success. Though diagnosing appendicitis can be tricky because the symptoms may mimic a number of conditions. Once the diagnosis is made and the appendix is successfully removed in surgery, the patient is cured. The outcome is successful, and many doctors view this success as a win.

Doctors also perceive losses when they struggle to diagnose complex conditions or treat chronic diseases. And, the greatest loss for doctors is the tragic death of a patient. From the doctor's perspective, the patient outcome is translated to the doctor's outcome. Surgeons often refer to their patients as "my gallbladder" or "my colectomy"; sometimes, the vision of the patient as a whole human being is lost.

From the Patient's Side of the Bed

Of course, patients want to be cured, too.

An exception is the patient with a rare psychiatric disease called Munchausen syndrome, who intentionally make and/or keep themselves sick to get their doctors' attention. A (fortunately) rarer group of patients who suffer from Munchausen's by proxy, harm their children to get attention. Our horror at these patients' acts speaks to the shared intention for cure.

However, in any given day, at any given doctor appointment, a patient may want something more or other than a "cure." Those needs may be physical or emotional. The success of an appointment is measured by how well that need is met on that day. Here are some things patients have told me are important in my twenty years as a physician, and my own experience as a patient and a family caregiver:

- "Make it stop hurting so much. Now."
- "Let me tell my story my way." Doctors often let patients speak for just seconds before they direct the conversation to efficiently gather information that directly leads to the diagnosis and treatment. Patients may want the relief of communicating worries and fears with someone they trust.
- "Answer my questions."
- "Help me make a tough choice."
- "See me as a person, not a collection of organs."
- "Remind me I am not alone in my suffering." All of us can tolerate pain. Pain that cannot be understood or managed leads to suffering. Suffering in silence as well as suffering in isolation is unbearable.

Patient-centered care means that the patient's agenda is listened to, heard, and satisfied.

Even when patients and physicians share a common vision of cure, they may be motivated by different incentives. Physicians are rewarded by the satisfaction that accompanies the elimination of suffering. (And, pragmatically, by the dollars they earn doing that task.) Patients long for an improved or extended life experience facilitated by optimal health. The patient's experience of health and illness is the unstated central agenda that drives compliance.

From the patient's side of the bed, cure is not enough. Patients want to he healed and whole. They want to know that they are not alone in their suffering. The healing comes from the sense that their lives are supported by someone who cares.

Unfortunately, our rapidly evolving technology may contribute to what one of my patients describes as "curing at the expense of healing." She said, "I told my doctor about 10 seconds of my story, then she interrupted and said she was going to order a CAT scan. That left me numb. I want to tell my story; it makes me feel better even when the listener doesn't say a word. My doctor doesn't want to listen; all she really wants to do is make a diagnosis. I'll take the warm caring touch of a doctor to a cold, hard CAT scan table any day."

The focus on physician-centered curing at the expense of patient-centered healing may contribute to our medical malpractice crisis. Imagine the physician for whom medicine is a zero-sum game. Cure means winning; bad outcomes and death mean losing. When things go wrong, some doctors may even pull back and steer clear of the patient with complications, an understandable extension of our human tendency to avoid mistakes and failures. Still, the seriously or critically ill patients are most in need of healing. They are most wounded by their doctor's perceived emotional abandonment or withdrawal. They interpret this withdrawal as evidence that the doctor made a mistake, and may respond by turning to the legal system for recompense.

THE MEDICAL HOME

Acknowledging the need for patient-centered care has led to the development of the "medical home." Our patients need no longer journey into the unfamiliar worlds of medicine alone without a guide. Organizations such as the American College of Physicians, the American Academy of Pediatrics, the American Osteopathic Association, and the American Academy of Family Physicians have developed an innovative concept called the medical home, which in essence identifies a primary care physician who would serve as a tour guide and companion for patients as they wend their way through the complex paths of healthcare services.

In February 2007, the organizations noted above released the Joint Principles of the Patient-Centered Medical Home, identifying the Patient-Centered Medical Home (PCMH) as "a healthcare setting that facilitates partnerships between individual patients, and their personal physicians, and when appropriate, the patient's family"(American Academy of Family Physicians [AAFP], 2007, p. 1).

Principles of the medical home identified in this document include (AAFP, 2007. pp. 1–2):

- ***Personal physician***—each patient has an ongoing relationship with a personal physician trained to provide first contact and continuous and comprehensive care.
- ***Physician directed medical practice***—the personal physician leads a team of individuals at the practice level who collectively take responsibility for the ongoing care of patients.
- ***Whole person orientation***—the personal physician is responsible for providing for all the patient's healthcare needs or taking responsibility for appropriately arranging care with other qualified professionals. This includes care for all stages of life, acute care, chronic care, preventive services, and end-of-life care.
- ***Care is coordinated and/or integrated*** across all elements of the complex healthcare system (e.g., subspecialty care, hospitals, home health agencies, nursing homes) and the patient's community (e.g., family, public and private community-based services). Care is facilitated by registries, information technology, health information exchange and other means to assure that patients get the indicated care when and where they need and want it in a culturally and linguistically appropriate manner.

The document identifies these hallmarks of the medical home that promote quality and safety (AAFP, 2007. pp. 1–2):

- Practices advocate for their patients to support the attainment of optimal, patient-centered outcomes that are defined by a care-planning process driven by a compassionate, robust partnership between physicians, patients, and the patient's family.
- Evidence-based medicine and clinical decision-support tools guide decision-making.
- Physicians in the practice accept accountability for continuous quality improvement through voluntary engagement in performance measurement and improvement.
- Patients actively participate in decision-making and feedback is sought to ensure patients' expectations are being met.
- Information technology is utilized appropriately to support optimal patient care, performance measurement, patient education, and enhanced communication.

- Practices go through a voluntary recognition process by an appropriate nongovernmental entity to demonstrate that they have the capabilities to provide patient centered services consistent with the medical home model.
- Patients and families participate in quality improvement activities at the practice level.

The Federal Centers for Medicare and Medicaid Services (CMS) have funded through 2009 demonstration projects based on the medical home concept in eight states with specific reimbursement systems and payment incentives (United States Department of Health and Human Services Centers for Medicare and Medicaid. H.R. 6111, 2006).

The medical home establishes and institutionalizes the patient–doctor partnership and encourages doctors to partner with patients and guide them through the unfamiliar world of healthcare services.

WHERE IS THE PATIENT'S VOICE?

If you want to buy a book, dine at a restaurant, or choose a vacation destination, you can find a breadth of reviews to guide your purchasing choices. Where do you go to find similar reviews of patients' experiences in the healthcare system? Tourist guides for the medical journey are few and far between. Would report cards about the medical outcomes of patients who seek care with a particular organization, hospital, or physician help patients as they venture into the world of medicine? I would say "no" because these outcomes are only one small component of the healthcare picture. Some other components that factor into finding the right healthcare provider are listed below:

- **Health care is a vehicle** to arrive at a destination of optimal patient health. Outcomes data measure how well a clinic, hospital, or physician safely arrives at this destination. Patient experience or patient satisfaction is a description of the ease and comfort of travel from the patient's perspective. Both sets of information support patient-centered quality care, and both are important, though, unfortunately, neither is easily accessible.
- **Patients want helpful information** to help them make practical day-to-day health-related choices—the new family in town looking for a

pediatrician; the woman deciding where to go for treatment of her breast cancer; the postal employee deciding whether to treat his low back pain with bed rest or an operation. Each individual's needs are different; these needs may not be identified or factored into report cards.

- **Patients' choices and behaviors influence overall health care outcomes and costs.** This is why, for better or for worse, drug companies invest billions of dollars in direct-to-consumer advertising. Patients' willingness to invest in health promotion (i.e., a healthy diet, regular exercise, and stress management) and follow doctors' orders directly correlates with healthcare costs. A doctor's skills and performance are not the only parameters that affect positive outcomes.
- **Poor patient compliance negatively impacts outcomes and increases health care costs.** Up to half of patients do not take medication as prescribed, make recommended lifestyle changes, or follow up as instructed by their doctors. Poor compliance or adherence translates to increased healthcare costs—and business costs—as healthy patients place themselves at increased risk for disease, chronic illnesses are exacerbated and recovery from acute illness is prolonged. Patient adherence can significantly affect outcome data.
- **Healthcare reform requires behavioral changes,** and most efforts are targeted at changes in healthcare delivery (the way doctors practice medicine). Efforts invested in supporting changes in patients' health-related behaviors reflect true innovation. Sharing of evidence-based best practices can be very helpful in promoting improved outcomes among healthcare organizations and institutions.
- **The voice of the patient is unheard.** Freud asked, "What do women really want?" I ask, "What do patients really want?" While we healthcare professionals may *think* we know what patients want or should want, it's easy to overlook the reality that patients and doctors enter and exit exam rooms with fundamental differences in perspectives, motivations, and expectations. Assessments of patient expectations and satisfaction are significant accountability and quality measures.
- **Seemingly trivial problems are huge barriers to quality, cost-effective healthcare delivery.** For example, patients' concerns about offending their doctors, on the surface, appear to be a minor issue; however, this is the main reason patients cite when explaining why they don't seek second medical opinions. Only one in five patients seek the

medical second opinions that result in a new diagnosis in as many as one in three cases. Those who do not may incur the cost of treatment for the wrong diagnosis.

- **Seemingly trivial changes in the way patients work with their doctors can yield huge benefits.** Three simple questions posed by coached hospitalized patients could help avoid preventable medical errors that prolong hospital stays, add medical expense, and take lives.
  - **What is that medication you're about to give me and what does it do?** To prevent medication errors.
  - **Do you know my name is Marge?** To prevent being the wrong patient transported to a test.
  - **Will you wash your hands?** To avoid preventable hospital-acquired infections.

HOW CAN PATIENTS ENHANCE DOCTOR–PATIENT COLLABORATION: SOME ADVICE FOR PATIENTS

You get the best, safest, and most cost-effective health care when you assume ultimate responsibility for your health. But do let your doctor be your doctor. Good health care is not an end in itself; rather, health care is a means to a healthy life best achieved in partnership with your doctor.

Ask not what your doctor can do for you; ask what you can do with your doctor.

Set Reasonable Expectations for Your Doctor

It would be great if doctors had the magical powers Dorothy sought from the Wizard of Oz. Here's what is behind the curtain of Dr. Oz.

- **Doctors are not mind readers.** Your doctors don't know what you think or how you feel. You must tell them. If, for example, your doctor does not seem concerned about your fatigue you can say, "Being tired all of the time is a big problem for me. I want to have more energy. I'm also worried that my fatigue could be a sign of cancer." There is no need to be embarrassed or shy; your doctor has heard it all before.
- **Doctors don't have crystal balls.** Have you asked a doctor a question like, "How long will my father live?" and gotten an answer like, "At his stage of disease there is a 70% chance for five-year survival."

That means that if there are 100 patients just like your dad, 70 will be alive in five years. Your real question is whether *your* father will be alive in five years. Statistics from clinical studies describe what happens with groups of people; they do not predict what will happen to an individual patient.

- **Doctors don't know everything.** Medical knowledge is advancing at an exploding rate, so no one person can keep up with everything. You may know more about your medical condition than your doctor does! Sometimes it's best to get a second opinion from a doctor who has a special interest in patients with your condition.
- **Doctors don't have 'The Answer.'** When you face a medical choice, there is no right answer. There is an answer that is best for you at that time in your life under those conditions. Your approach to snoring may be different than you neighbor's.
- **Doctors don't have magic wands.** The miracle drug that offers a cure without any risk simply doesn't exist. Complications from aspirin take more lives than AIDS each year. Make sure you know the possible risks before you agree to any treatment, including herbal remedies. And be suspicious of any product that claims to offer a cure for a wide variety of illnesses.
- **Doctors spend a limited amount of time with you.** Most doctors are employed by clinics or hospitals, and they are expected to meet productivity goals defined by their employers. That means your doctor is expected to see a certain number of patients each day and spend a limited amount of time with each patient. Frequently it does not seem like enough time to you and to your doctor. Prepare for your appointments so you can make the most of the time you have. Write a list of questions. Ask for a longer appointment when needed, even if it means paying for the time out of your pocket.
- **Doctors make mistakes.** The Institute of Medicine estimates up to 98,000 patients died in the hospital in 1999 as a result of preventable medical errors. That is more patients than died from car accidents or breast cancer in the same year. Medical errors represent the eighth leading cause of death in the United States. This isn't about bad doctors. Mistakes happen because the healthcare system is complex, health care is delivered by people, and people make mistakes. The title of the Institute's report is "To Err is Human." Proactive and vigilant participation in your health care is your best protection.

- **Doctors are people, too.** Doctors get angry, sad, and frustrated just like you do. The reaction from your doctor may be a response to something other than you. A doctor who seems impatient might be thinking about the critically ill patient in the ER. A doctor who asks you the same question twice may have just received a worrisome call from a family member.
- **You have a job, too.** The action plan you and your doctor create is an unwritten contract. Honor your doctor and yourself by honoring the contract. Let your doctor know if the plan isn't working and renegotiate.

Your Role

Know Your Story and Tell It

Story-telling plays a central role in your partnership with your doctor. Your doctor's question—"How do you feel?"—is your doctor's way of saying, "Tell me your story." Your doctor can diagnose your medical condition most of the time just by listening. Your unique health story includes the events that occurred in your body, your experience of those events, and the way in which you bring meaning to them. Capture your story in your own words so your story makes sense to you.

Maintain Copies of Your Medical Records

Good medical care is based on access to complete and accurate medical information. The best way to assure that your doctor has the complete record is for you to bring it with you to the appointment. You have a right to gain access to your medical record. Just call the office and say, "How do I get copies of my medical records?" Bring a self-addressed stamped envelope to each appointment and request that records and lab reports be sent to you.

Ask Your Doctor About Lifestyle Choices

At each visit, ask your doctor to identify lifestyle choices that support your health goals. Do not mistake early diagnosis for true prevention. If the answer to the question, "How do I prevent colon cancer?" is to "get a colonoscopy and pay attention to changes in your bowel habits," then you have just been given a recipe for early detection of cancer. Don't settle only for this approach. Ask, "What do I do to prevent the development of colon cancer instead of just detecting it early? What diet do you recommend? What about exercise or a daily aspirin?"

Set Reasonable Expectations for Yourself

Expect that you won't be at your best when you're sick. You don't have your normal stamina and your mind may be clouded by pain or medication. Times of illness are times in which you face three frightening conditions: pain, disability, and death. Many feel like helpless children when they're sick. Plan for fear. Expect you will not hear or absorb most of what your doctor tells you, so bring a friend and your personal health journal with your medical records and a pad of paper to each appointment with your doctor. Tell your doctor what scares you. And don't worry alone. Give yourself a break if you feel like a frightened kid wanting your doctor to step in and take care of everything, like your parents did. It's normal.

Manage Medical Information

Information is powerful medicine. Just as with any other medication, you need to take the right dose. Take too much and you can experience toxic effects. Take too little and you will not experience its benefits. Identify your own optimal dose of medical information. One patient said to me, "Doc, I don't want to hear about side effects. I'll get every one." Another patient came with a file box heavy with her research. Remember that no Food and Drug Administration (FDA)-like organization regulates the quality of medical information. Anyone can say anything on the Internet, so be careful of your sources. Last, let your doctor translate clinical studies and customize medical recommendations to you and your own life.

Make Smart Medical Choices

When it comes right down to it, your job as a patient is to make medical choices that best serve you. Informed consent is not a form you sign; it is the process of making informed medical choices by weighing the risks and benefits of a plan, and comparing different options. Your medical choices fall on your shoulders for several reasons. First, you know your own risk tolerance and your perception of benefits. For some the side effect of nausea is a mild annoyance while for others it's agony. Second, you live with the consequences of your choices. Get the help and support of your doctor all along the way. In fact, you may choose to let the doctor decide, especially if the patient is your child or aging parent.

Recognize Promising Frontiers

In the spirit of "walking my own talk" of noticing what's right, here are some revolutionary developments that are still in fledgling stages. These ideas will contribute to a better healthcare system in years to come.

- *Evidence-based medicine:* A gray-haired doctor greeted my medical school class with this thought, "About 50% of what you're about to learn is wrong; unfortunately, we don't know which 50%." Your doctor carries out many medical practices because that's the way it's always been done. Now, doctors are turning to science to answer the question, "Does this intervention really help patients?"
- *Quality-of-life data:* Traditional clinical studies measure outcomes such as length of life and complication rates. Most patients want to know if a medical intervention will help them live better lives, qualitatively and quantitatively. Clinical study designs increasingly include quality-of-life measurements.
- *Clinical performance reports:* Doctors' outcomes vary, and generally you get better outcomes from doctors who treat higher volumes of patients like you. Evolving outcomes reports will help you select the best provider for your care.
- *Genomics:* Genomics, the diagnosis and treatment of disease on a genetic level, offers a mechanism to intervene at an early stage before disease damages organs. While we still face technical and ethical concerns, this field holds great promise.

HOW CAN DOCTORS ENHANCE PATIENT–DOCTOR COLLABORATION? SUGGESTIONS FOR HEALTH CARE PROVIDERS

To get the answers that help patients make better choices, doctors have to ask the right questions. To influence patient behavior, healthcare providers need to understand what is important to patients. To enhance patient–doctor collaboration, healthcare providers should:

- **Begin to engage patients in a dialogue** and ask, "What information would help you make better healthcare choices?" This could begin with open-ended telephone surveys or even a Web site to which patients offer input and suggestions. Ideas collected from this effort could direct the development of a formal patient-centered survey tool that could become an industry standard for benchmarking.
- **Reframe patient feedback.** For patients deciding on a new doctor, answers to judgment questions like "How much do you like your doctor?" or "How good is your doctor?" are of questionable value. Without an understanding of the expectations of the reviewer, it is difficult to decide on the information's relevance. The most successful and satisfied patients enjoy a good fit between what they want and need from their doctors and what the doctors are able to offer. No doctor or clinic can be all things to all people. Defining a clinic's strengths and the profile of its successful and satisfied patients can allow patients to opt for a clinic or doctor that matches their needs and expectations.
- **Create patient-centered interventions and measure results.** The barrier to health-related behavioral changes is not always the lack of information. Even when patients know that they should get second medical opinions, ask for explanations in English, and ask embarrassing medical questions, they don't do it because they don't have the skills to implement these tasks. Mentoring and coaching patients in the collaborative process can allow them to improve their skills and enhance the collaboration.

CONCLUSION

Behind every clinical goal is a person, with his or her own personal goals. Healthcare providers should consider the perspectives of their patient partners throughout the patient–doctor collaboration to enhance the benefits and outcomes of these collaborations.

My advice to my fellow doctors and other healthcare professionals?

- Remember: patients aren't getting excited about that drop in blood pressure; they're excited about living long enough to walk their daughters down the aisle.
- Commit to being a better listener; with each other as well as with patients.

- Ask the patient what he or she wants. "What do we need to accomplish today for you to go home and say, 'That was a good appointment?'"
- Define health outcomes and monitor progress toward their achievement together with your patient.
- Remember that health choices are made with emotion, not logic. Your expertise and guidance is important, but embarrassment, fear, and past medical experiences shape the patients' perspectives and choices.
- Respect personal and cultural differences in health beliefs and practices.
- When patients are more satisfied, *you* are more satisfied.

We are moving towards the broader adoption of patient-centered health care. An investment in understanding the patient's perspective, coupled with an invitation to our patients to more fully participate in the increasingly prevalent and unique patient–doctor partnerships, offer one of the most promising frontiers in the transformation of our healthcare system.

DISCUSSION QUESTIONS

1. How do patients' and doctors' perspectives differ?
2. What are the "job descriptions" for patients and for doctors?
3. What can patients do to collaborate more effectively with their doctors?
4. What can doctors do to ensure that their patients' needs and expectations are met?
5. Would patient reviews of doctors (i.e., "report cards") be a good idea?
6. How might a medical home concept benefit quality of care?

REFERENCES

American Academy of Family Physicians (2007). *Joint Principles of the Patient Center Medical Home*. Retrieved October 12, 2008 from http://www.aafp.org/online/etc/medialib/aafp_org/documents/policy/fed/jointprinciplespcmh0207.Par.0001.File.tmp/022107medicalhome.pdf

Consumer Reports. Retrieved November 2, 2008 from http://www.consumersunion.org/pub/core_health_care/004153.html

United States Department of Health and Human Services Centers for Medicare and Medicaid. (2006). H.R. 6111, *Tax Relief and Health Act of 2006*. Retrieved October 12, 2008 from http://www.cms.hhs.gov/PQRI/Downloads/PQRITaxReliefHealthCareAct.pdf

CHAPTER 5

Interprofessional Collaboration: A Nursing Perspective

Nancy Spector, PhD, RN

LEARNING OBJECTIVES

After completing the chapter, the reader will be able to:

1. Explain the importance of collaboration among healthcare professions.
2. Discuss the principles of interprofessional collaboration as applied to nursing.
3. Identify the barriers to interprofessional collaboration that are specific to nursing.
4. Discuss how enhancing collaboration in health care can improve patient safety.
5. Apply the principles of collaboration to two case studies.
6. Describe how nursing education programs might integrate collaborative competencies throughout the curriculum.

KEY TERMS

Interprofessional
Collaboration
Nursing

Communication
Barriers
Interdisciplinary
Principles

INTRODUCTION

Since nursing's a teamwork vocation
With science and art its foundation,
Is it too much to ask
In this admirable task
That we focus on collaboration?

This chapter presents the interprofessional collaboration from a nursing perspective. This approach may seem counterintuitive for a book that is promoting more interdisciplinary communication, mutual decision-making, and less working in silos. However, each of the professions approaches collaboration with its own perspective. Understanding these perspectives is critical to making interprofessional collaborations successful.

WHAT IS INTERPROFESSIONAL COLLABORATION?

Highly complex health systems require frequent interaction between many different professionals (Arford, 2005; Garman, Leach, & Spector, 2006). Working in isolation is no longer a functional option. This section will explore the various definitions of interprofessional collaboration and its associated terminology.

Interprofessional Versus Interdisciplinary

In the nursing literature, the term *interprofessional education* is preferred to *multidisciplinary* or *interdisciplinary education*. According to Barnsteiner, Disch, Hall, Mayer, and Moore (2007), the term interdisciplinary is often understood by physicians as collaboration among physician specialties. Further, multidisciplinary education describes student learning in a parallel fashion. An example of interdisciplinary education would be medical students studying many medical disciplines such as obstetrics, psychiatry, internal medicine, etc. Interprofessional education refers to healthcare students studying among various professions, such as nursing, medicine, pharmacy, etc. Cullen, Fraser, and Symonds (2003) define multiprofessional learning as two or more professions studying common content together, but without interaction between the groups. Others see interprofessional learning as an umbrella term for a variety of professions studying together (O'Halloran, Hean, Humphris & MacLeod-Clark, 2006). Cullen et al. (2003) use the interprofessional education terminology because it focuses on understanding each others' roles and working together. As a rule, in interprofessional learning there is interaction between the groups.

An example of multiprofessional learning with minimal interaction occurred during the author's graduate nursing education. When we took physiology class with the medical students, there was almost no interaction between the groups. The medical students had assigned a lead note-taker to take notes that were ultimately distributed to the entire class. The medical students had agreed to share these notes with the nursing students, but had not allowed the nursing graduate students to be lead note-takers. Fortunately, research has shown the benefits of interprofessional learning and study, and the practice has become more common in recent years.

Collaboration

According to the *Oxford English Dictionary* (2008), the words *collaboration* and *collaborate* derive from the Latin word, *collaborare*, with *col* meaning together and *laborare* meaning to work. The OED's definition is "To work in conjunction with another or others, to co-operate; *esp.* in a literary or artistic production, or the like." The first entry for *collaborate* is from 1871, while that for *collaboration* is from 1860.

The health care and nursing literature have a wealth of information on collaboration, including many different definitions of the word. Probably the strictest and most *avant-garde* definition comes from Tom Wolff, who calls collaboration an overused word. He cites Himmelman's definition of collaboration (Wolff, 2005), which builds on networking, coordination, and cooperation. According to Himmelman and Wolff, successful collaborators must enhance the capacity of the group for mutual benefit, and achieve a common goal by sharing risks, resources, responsibilities, and rewards. Himmelman's definition of coordination is when professionals exchange information and alter activities for mutual benefit and for a mutual purpose. Cooperation includes everything included in coordination, but adds the sharing of resources and changes "altering" activities to "modifying" activities. True collaboration has the potential of creating and promoting major changes. Himmelman and Wolff describe it as a "radical concept," which takes time and dedication to achieve. From their perspective, most instances of interprofessional collaboration that are described in the literature fall into their categories of cooperation or coordination.

Most researchers (see Table 5-1) use a broader definition of collaboration in which striving for a common goal (Himmelman's "mutual purpose") is key.

Zarenstein and Bryant (2000), in their systematic review of interventions to promote collaboration between physicians and nurses, define collaboration as nurses and physicians working jointly and sharing responsibility for the care of patients. Collaboration is evidenced, according to Zarenstein and Bryant (2000), when joint decision-making occurs, when there are frequent adaptations to meet patient needs, and when there are rapid changes in the allocation of tasks between professionals. Lindeke and Sieckert (2005) discuss the multidimensional aspects of collaboration that include face-to-face encounters, along with e-mail and voice mail. But, collaboration is more than a one-way or two-way information exchange. It is more complex, requiring mutual respect and mutual commitment among collaborators.

However, Barnsteiner et al. (2007) present evidence that nurses and physicians may define teamwork and collaboration differently. While nurses commonly describe it as including shared decision-making, some physicians define it as having their needs anticipated and directions followed. McCool (2004) adds another variable as he explores interprofessional collaboration in today's competitive society. For example, universities, hospitals and physicians are rated annually by *U.S. News and World Report*, thus promoting the race to be "number 1." How, McCool asks, can we cooperate in this highly-charged atmosphere of competition? A recognition of the benefits of collaboration within the healthcare organization's culture is a first step.

> *Definition of Interprofessional Collaboration:*
>
> A complex process through which relationships are developed among healthcare professionals so that they effectively interact and work together for the mutual goal of safe and quality patient care.

Table 5-1. Definitions of Collaboration

Definition	Citation
"Collaboration is perceived as working together toward a common goal."	Boswell & Cannon (2005).
This author conceptualizes collaboration as both a process (a series of events) and an outcome (a synthesis of different perspectives).	Gardner (2005), p. 2.
"Collaboration is a complex process that requires intentional sharing and joint responsibility for patient care."	Lindeke & Sieckert (2005), p. 1.
". . . collaboration will be defined as an interdisciplinary process of problem solving, shared responsibility for decision making, and the ability to carry out a plan of care while working toward a common goal."	McKay & Crippen (2008), p. 110.
"Collaboration is best viewed as a relationship, a process consisting of ongoing interactions."	Schmalenberg et al. (2005), p. 450.
Collaboration enhances "the capacity of the other, for mutual benefit and to achieve a common goal by sharing risks, resources, responsibilities and rewards."	Wolff (2005; citing Himmelman's definition).
"Collaboration means 'to work jointly'. For nurses and doctors sharing responsibility for the care of a patient, collaboration was taken to mean sharing of information, coordination of work, and joint decision-making on aspects of patient care."	Zarenstein & Bryant (2000), p. 2.

An agreement on the definition of interprofessional collaboration is essential, because the definition shapes the pedagogical approaches and curricula for academic programs in healthcare education (O'Halloran et al., 2006).

WHY IS INTERDISCIPLINARY COLLABORATION IMPORTANT IN NURSING?

The Evidence

In 2000, the Institute of Medicine (IOM) published the alarming report, *To Err is Human: Building a Safer Health System* (Kohn, Corrigan, & Donaldson, 2000). The report summarized identified problems with patient safety in the United States, and recommended the improvement of safety systems in health care. One recommendation was to pay more attention to interdisciplinary practice. A year later, the IOM's *Crossing the Quality Chasm* presented 10 rules for redesigning healthcare systems (IOM, 2001). One of the rules was that clinicians and institutions should actively collaborate and communicate to ensure the exchange of information and optimal coordination of care. Then, in 2003, the IOM published *Health Professions Education: A Bridge to Quality* (Greiner & Knebel, 2003), which called for redesigning education for health professionals. Their vision for the 21st century was that "all professionals should be educated to deliver patient-centered care as members of an interdisciplinary team, emphasizing evidence-based practice, quality improvement approaches, and informatics." (p. 3) These IOM reports made it clear that the future of healthcare education and practice should include an increased focus on interdisciplinary collaboration.

Does interdisciplinary collaboration make a difference in patient outcomes? It certainly is reasonable to conclude that cooperatively working together will improve professionals' effectiveness (Barnsteiner et al., 2007).

One of the first studies to find improved outcomes with collaboration was Knaus, Draper, Wagner, and Zimmerman (1986). Decreased patient mortality was noted when nurses and physicians had collaborative relationships. Other studies have reported a positive impact on patient safety and a reduction in errors when there is effective interprofessional collaboration (Silver & Antonow, 2000; Weeks, Mills, Dittus, Aron, & Batalden, 2001). There also are reports of increased nursing job satisfaction and retention as well as improved teamwork when interprofessional collaboration is effectively integrated into healthcare systems (Abramson & Mizrahi, 1996; Baggs & Ryan, 1990).

The Cochrane Collaboration (2008) is "an international not-for-profit and independent organization, dedicated to making up-to-date, accurate information about the effects of healthcare readily available worldwide" (p. 1). It produces and disseminates systematic reviews of healthcare interventions and promotes the search for evidence in the form of clinical trials and other studies of interventions. Two studies for the Collaboration analyzed the outcomes of interventions that promoted collaboration between nurses and physicians (Zarenstein & Bryant, 2000) and the effects of interprofessional education on practice and healthcare outcomes (Zarenstein et al., 2000). Using the Cochrane Collaboration's strict inclusion criteria for study validity, Zarenstein and Bryant (2000) found 31 studies to be potentially relevant, and 2 met their criteria. They found moderate gains in patient stays and in-cost savings when interprofessional collaboration between doctors and nurses occurred. In Zarenstein et al. (2000) no studies met their criteria. However, the authors expanded their criteria to gain insight into interprofessional education (Barr, Koppel, Reeves, Hammick & Freeth, 2005). Positive outcomes noted were increased collaborative behavior and improved communication and cooperation.

Most authors agree that there is a need for more research on the outcomes of interprofessional collaboration and effective strategies for promoting it in training and practice. Steinert (2005) points to a gap in research in the areas of faculty development and instructional implementation. There is also agreement that more rigorously conducted studies and multimethod studies are needed that utilize appropriate evaluation methodologies and valid and reliable measurement instruments. New research should focus on assessing long-term outcomes rather than on relaying self-reports of student experiences (Barnsteiner et al., 2007; Glen, 2004; Glen & Reeves, 2004; MacKay, 2004; Mendez, Armayor, Navarlaz, & Wakefield, 2008). Stone (2006) advocates for a triangulation of methods, including both qualitative and quantitative studies in future research.

Requirements for Interprofessional Collaboration in Nursing Education

To best understand the requirements for integrating interprofessional collaboration into nursing programs, a review of how nurses are educated in the United States is necessary. There is significant heterogeneity in U.S. nursing education and practice. Garman et al. (2006) analyze the selection of nursing students, the nursing curriculum and training, and the career paths of nurses as compared to other healthcare professionals. There are multiple options for students interested in nursing to consider:

- Licensed Practical or Vocational Nurse
- Associate Degree Nursing
- Registered Nurse
- Bachelor of Science in Nursing
- Master's of Science in Nursing, including Nurse Practitioner programs, Clinical Nurse Specialist and Clinical Nurse Leader programs.
- Doctoral programs, including Doctor of Nursing Practice, Doctor of Nursing Science, and PhD.

National accreditation in nursing, through one of two accrediting agencies, is voluntary for nursing education programs. The National League for Nursing Accrediting Commission (NLNAC) accredits all licensed practical nursing, diploma, associate degree, baccalaureate degree, master's, and doctor's (DNP) nursing programs. The Commission on Collegiate Nursing Education (CCNE) accredits all baccalaureate, master's, and DNP programs. In addition, to ensure compliance with high standards by all programs, state Boards of Nursing (or in two states, Higher Education) approve nursing programs as well.

Is interprofessional collaboration a requirement for nursing programs? Table 5-2 describes how the CCNE, NLNAC, and the Nursing Boards' regulations require that programs incorporate interprofessional collaboration in their programs.

The next question is whether nursing programs utilize interprofessional education. More research is needed in this area, but two national studies show that the implementation of true interprofessional education is minimal. In 2006, the National Council of State Boards of Nursing (NCSBN) conducted a national study of nursing education, investigating how 410 U.S. nursing programs taught nurses. One aim of the study was to identify elements of nursing education that lead to better preparation of new nurse graduates. The NCSBN studied 7497 nurses who attended the 410 nursing programs and assessed their achievement of learning outcomes. The results showed that, while 58.6% of the RN programs reported having multiprofessional clinical activities, most likely these experiences were "parallel play" type of experiences, as described in the above section. Only 23.2% of the new nurses reported taking any kind of coursework along with other

Table 5-2. Accreditation and Regulatory Requirements for Interprofessional Collaboration in Prelicensure Programs

Organization	Requirement
Commission on Collegiate Nursing Education (CCNE)	Utilize *Essentials of Baccalaureate Education for Professional Nursing Practice* (draft document; American Association of Colleges of Nursing, 2008): Essential VI: "Inter-professional Communication and Collaboration for Improving Patient Health Outcomes" (p. 22).
National League for Nursing Accrediting Commission (NLNAC)	Standard 4: Curriculum (for practical nursing, associate degree, diploma, and baccalaureate programs): "4.6 The curriculum and instructional processes reflect educational theory, interdisciplinary collaboration, research, and best practice standards while allowing for innovation, flexibility, and technological advances." (NLNAC, 2008)
National Council of State Boards of Nursing (NCSBN) Model Administrative Rules for Education	Curriculum: "1) (d) Coursework including, but not limited to: (04) Working in interdisciplinary teams to cooperate, collaborate, communicate and integrate client care and health promotion." (NCSBN, 2004)

healthcare professionals. Significantly, new nurses had difficulty knowing when and how to call physicians when there were questions or problems. New nurses who reported that they were not able to work effectively with the healthcare team were 2.2 times more likely to have difficulty in their professional practice. These findings underlined the importance of competency in interprofessional collaboration.

Preliminary results from another national study from the Carnegie Foundation found that there are almost no interprofessional learning or practice opportunities taking place in prelicensure nursing education. Therefore, one of their recommendations was for nursing educators to deliberately include interprofessional teaching in class and in clinical experiences (personal communication: Dr. Patricia Benner, lead researcher for the study).

Some have advocated for the nursing licensure exam (NCLEX) to incorporate questions about interprofessional collaboration, thinking that this would foster its inclusion in curricula. However, federal law mandates that a high-stakes examination, allowing a candidate to work in a particular field, should be based on current standards of practice. Changes in nursing education must therefore be incorporated into practice standards before they will appear on the NCLEX. Unfortunately, well-intentioned suggestions in the literature, such as the following, may be ineffective: "Finally, get active with the National Council of State Boards of Nursing and other health professions' licensing boards to request that there be questions on the exams related to understanding the impact of interprofessional collaboration on health care outcomes" (Barnsteiner et al., 2007, p. 149). No specialty group, or other groups with specific agendas, can lobby NCSBN to put questions on the NCLEX. Changes would be driven only by analyses of assessment data from the first six months of nursing practice.

Barriers to Interprofessional Collaboration in Nursing

There is research evidence that interprofessional collaboration improves outcomes, but it isn't yet occurring regularly in nursing education. Why not? The healthcare environment itself can be seen as a barrier to interprofessional collaboration. For example, because of the current nursing shortage, nurses have increased workloads, fewer resources, and less support, limiting optimal collaboration (McKay & Crippen, 2008). Reluctance of other disciplines to participate in a collaborative opportunity is also a barrier. Reeves et al. (2006) described a project that offered interprofessional education to two community mental health teams. Unfortunately, there was poor participation among the medical staff, undermining the opportunity for interprofessional collaboration. To promote such a project's success, the researchers noted, senior management support for participation within each discipline is critical.

Rigid organizational structures and hierarchies are also barriers in the healthcare industry that impede successful collaboration (Erickson, McHarney-Brown, Seeger & Kaufman, 1998; Mendez et al., 2008). The example above from the NCSBN study of nursing education, in which new nurses reported that they often graduated not knowing how or when to call the physician, demonstrates the effect of training programs not allowing student nurses to call physicians. Without this experience, nursing students do not have an opportunity to learn and practice this skill. These study findings were presented at an interprofessional invitational meeting at NCSBN in 2006. Discussion on this issue revealed that clinical facilities commonly yielded to physician requests not to be bothered by students asking questions, reflecting hierarchical structure. To promote interprofessional collaboration, a system change would be needed to enlist physicians in nurse training.

The educational environment itself can often be rigid and complex, thereby becoming a barrier to interprofessional collaboration (Cullen et al., 2003). To address the nursing shortage, student enrollment has been increased but frequently without an associated increase in faculty hiring. Faculty burdened by overcrowded classes find it difficult to develop and implement unique interprofessional experiences. Additionally, changing curricula to include interprofessional education can be challenging, requiring much discussion and negotiation among nursing faculty. When other disciplines are included, the challenges of aligning curricula and schedules can be daunting.

Another barrier to interprofessional collaboration has been the historical hierarchy in the healthcare setting that identified physicians as the most powerful professionals (Garman et al., 2006; McKay & Crippen, 2008). The active participation and demonstrated value of nurse providers and specialists on the healthcare team have begun to guide the traditional power structure towards the modern model of an egalitarian partnership.

Additional barriers to a productive healthcare environment are the reported intimidating and disruptive behaviors of health professionals. The Joint Commission has recently addressed this issue, and they report that these "bad behaviors" foster medical errors, contribute to poor patient satisfaction and adverse outcomes, increase the costs of care, and cause qualified professionals to leave health care (The Joint Commission, 2008). One recent study of nurse leaders reports that of 1377 respondents, representing every region of the United States and 17 countries, an alarming 80% surveyed have experienced some form of violence in the work setting (Hader, 2008). This has become such a problem for healthcare systems that on July 9, 2008, The Joint Commission sent out a Sentinel Event Alert, and established a new Leadership standard (LD.03.01.01) that addresses disruptive and inappropriate behaviors:

- EP 4: The hospital/organization has a code of conduct that defines acceptable and disruptive and inappropriate behaviors.

- EP 5: Leaders create and implement a process for managing disruptive and inappropriate behaviors.

Further, The Joint Commission recommends that healthcare settings take 11 specific steps (The Joint Commission, 2008), including educating the healthcare team members about professional behavior with specifics, such as being courteous during telephone interactions, business etiquette, and general "people skills."

Significant differences have been identified as well in the culture and content of medical vs. nursing education. Garman et al. (2006) reported significant differences in areas such as how nurses and physicians are educated, why each student group selected their chosen profession, and their expectations for rewards. There were differences in function among the two groups as well: Nursing students often formed tight, collaborative clinical groups, whereas medical students often studied or worked alone. In highly competitive environments, some medical students had actually been discovered to have actively sabotaged others' work.

In the clinical setting, role confusion, territorialism and professional rivalry are additional contributors to this barrier to effective collaboration (Mendez et al., 2008). Contributing to a power imbalance, nurses are typically employed by the hospital, while physicians are part of what Garman et al. (2006) term the *dealer network* employed by their patients. Healthcare organizations may respond to perceived customer demands by acceding to their doctors' requests, resulting in an uneven playing field between nurses and physicians. Lindeke & Sieckert (2005) suggest that one way of reducing this power differential would be to eliminate using titles for members of a healthcare team, thereby neutralizing the unequal playing field. As more and more nurse specialists obtain doctoral degrees, the issue of parity should continue to improve.

Barriers can arise because healthcare professionals, due to education, culture, or temperament, often have different perspectives (Garman et al., 2006). For example, nurses are often socialized to arrive at a consensus, physicians focus on 'the right answer' and want to rule out alternatives, and administrators are guided by a business model (Lindeke & Sieckert, 2005). With respect to trust and honesty in professional relationships, Schmalenberg et al. (2005) assert that physicians tend to be *iffers*, while nurses are *untillers*. That is, physicians say, "if you meet my expectations, I will trust you," while nurses say, "I'll trust you until I can't." Understanding these perspectives can be quite helpful when collaborating among different disciplines.

In one study examining communication barriers among healthcare personnel, the researchers explored the relationship styles of nurses and physicians (Coeling & Wilcox, 1994). They found that physicians focused more on the content of the message, while nurses placed more importance on the relationship aspect of the message. Similarly, Schmalenberg et al. (2005) suggested that physicians want messages delivered in bullets and may be stressed by time-consuming narratives. It is possible that, as approximately 92% of nurses are women, some of these communication differences may be gender-related. Gardner (2005) suggested that learning more about cross-gender communications might provide data to help strengthen interprofessional collaboration.

Principles for Interprofessional Collaboration

The literature is awash with information and resources that can serve as foundations for successful interprofessional collaboration in nursing and health care. Table 5-3 is a summary of published guidelines by experts in the field. Additional detail is available in their articles.

However, the general principles of effective interprofessional collaboration, as identified by a literature review and supplemented by the author from her experience, can be summarized as below.

1. For successful collaboration, a **shared vision** is essential. In health care, one shared vision might be "delivery of consumer-centered, quality care." The Oregon Consortium for Nursing Education (OCNE) is an exemplar for collaboration and will be discussed in the next section. OCNE's shared vision is a "Commitment to excellence and innovation, in our effort to serve and promote the Health of All Oregonians." (OCNE, 2008) All of OCNE's collaborative partners are familiar with and share this vision, which binds the initiatives of its different nursing programs towards a common goal.
2. Developing **trust and respect** for each other is also essential for effective collaboration, and must be a core value of a collaborative organization. Expertise and competence among team members is essential for professionals to successfully develop trust and respect for each other (Schmalenberg, Kramer, King, and Krugman, 2005). In their investigation of evidence-based practices to enable interdisciplinary

Table 5-3. Guidelines for Developing Interprofessional Collaboration Learning Experiences

Guidelines	Study
Criteria for full engagement of interprofessional education • Explicit philosophy • Interprofessional faculty co-create learning experiences • Students learn how collaboration promotes safe, quality care • Learning experiences are embedded in the curriculum and as part of caseload • Demonstrated competence by students with a single set of interprofessional competencies (such as IOMs) • Organizational infrastructure and support	Barnsteiner et al., 2007
Characteristics of successful collaboration • Networking • Leadership • Vision	Boswell & Cannon, 2005
Essential competencies of collaboration • Know thyself • Learn to value and manage diversity • Develop constructive conflict resolution skills • Use your power to create win–win situations • Master interpersonal and process skills • Leverage multidisciplinary forums to increase collaboration • Appreciate that collaboration can occur spontaneously • Balance autonomy and unity in collaborative relationships • Remember that collaboration is not required for all decisions	Gardner, 2005

(continues)

Table 5-3. Guidelines for Developing Interprofessional Collaboration Learning Experiences (continued)

Guidelines	**Study**
Self-development strategies • Develop emotional maturity • Understand the perspectives of others • Avoid compassion fatigue Team-development strategies • Build the team • Negotiate respectfully • Manage conflict wisely • Avoid negative behaviors • Design facilities for collaboration Communication-development strategies • Communicate effectively in emergencies • Use electronic communication thoughtfully	Lindeke & Sieckert, 2005
Questions for educators • When to introduce students to this? • How long should the initiative last? • Best learning methods? • Which disciplines should be included? • What resources needed? How to maintain budget? Types of learning (methods are included) • Exchange-based • Observation-based • Action-based • Simulation-based • Practice-based	Mendez et al., 2008

(continues)

Table 5-3. Guidelines for Developing Interprofessional Collaboration Learning Experiences (continued)

Guidelines	Study

Steps in development of a curriculum model
• Identify common content
• Decide between common learning vs. interprofessional learning
• Identify a model of learning (process)
  • guided discovery learning
  • collaborative learning
  • interprofessional learning
  • combination: facilitated collaborative interprofessional learning
• Integrated curriculum content (the "what" of learning)
	O'Halloran et al., 2006

Faculty development strategies
• Aim to bring change to individual and organizational level
• Target diverse stakeholders
• Content:
  • interprofessional education
  • teaching and learning
  • leadership and organizational change
• Variety of settings, using diverse formats
• Model principles of interprofessional education
• Incorporate principles of effective educational design
• Adoption of a dissemination model (develop "champions")
	Steinert, 2005

Interprofessional capabilities (specific capabilities are listed under each in the article) • Ethical practice • Knowledge in practice • Interprofessional working • Reflection	Walsh, Gordon, Marshall, Wilson, & Hunt, 2005

collaboration, they observed that physicians judged competence by how well nurses gave reports, particularly in emergent situations. Nurses, they found, judged physician competence by evaluating patient outcomes, lack of complications, whether physicians sought out nurses before writing orders, and how physicians listened and collaborated with nurses and other healthcare professionals in the plan of care. Both nurses and physicians consider clinical certification as a valuable measure of competence.

3. **Understanding each other's perspectives** is also key for effective interprofessional collaboration. The original discussion about differences in communication styles is relevant to this principle. Each professional will carry a different mental model about how the collaboration will proceed (Gardner, 2005). When healthcare professionals recognize and understand their differences, they will be able to reflect about these mental models and get to know themselves and others better. Lindeke & Sieckert (2005) assert that when different perspectives are brought to the table, creative and practical solutions may develop that wouldn't have come about if the collaborative team had a homogenous perspective. The result: a positive outcome. If challenges in moving forward together arise, the team can review their shared vision and reasons for collaboration to reestablish their common goals.
4. Conflicts are not surprising when different cultures attempt to work together. Successful **conflict resolution** can help collaborative teams overcome differences and regain momentum (Gardner, 2005). As previously noted, nurses more often strive for consensus, while other healthcare professionals may prefer other modes of interaction, setting up a conflict early in the collaboration. Additionally, the foundations and cultures of the major health professional groups (Garman et al., 2006) are very different for varied healthcare professionals. These elements include key identifying principles, career choice influences, admission requirements to education, education preparation, and expectations for rewards. Conversation workshops among the member groups in a collaboration may allow the sharing of perspectives, agendas, and expected goals and begin the process of developing a common vision and outcomes. Outstanding leadership is a cornerstone for the success of this process. As Lindeke & Sieckert (2005) write, encouraging conflict resolution without destroying group cohesiveness requires maturity, humility, and excellent facilitation skills.

5. **System support** is another essential principle underpinning successful interprofessional collaboration. Facility design, adequate resources, and support from upper administration are required for interprofessional collaboration to effectively take place. The facility should be designed to include adequate space, layout, and convenience, and provide secure areas for private conversations. But, Erickson et al. (1998) suggest that often the cited barriers of institutional nonsupport are more conceptual than real. The institutions may not understand the benefits of collaboration on patient outcomes, may lack a clear vision that supports interdisciplinary collaboration, or may perceive a financial disincentive in the process. Legislative and policy initiatives, and external and internal funding, can encourage the implementation and support of intraprofessional collaboration (Erickson et al., 1998). For example, The Joint Commission's 2008 standards for addressing disruptive behavior in the workplace setting should benefit interprofessional collaboration.
6. **Effective communication and interpersonal skills** are needed to promote all of these functions. These skills and styles vary from person to person, and may be influenced by professional training and culture. Skills that nurses may find particularly useful in the collaborative setting are communicating clearly, confidently, and assertively. Feedback from peers can help to strengthen these skills, and nurses must be reflective in their self-assessment (Arford, 2005). Other skills nurses may find helpful are flexibility and the ability to tolerate ambiguity. In order to work collaboratively with others, the nurse also must develop systems thinking, which is the ability to see the contextual situation from the perspective of the whole system (Gardner, 2005).

CASE STUDIES: DECONSTRUCTING TWO EXAMPLES

An Example Where Effective Interprofessional Collaboration Did Not Take Place

The following is a situation from the author's educational experience. The interactions included representatives from both nursing and medicine, but, unfortunately, there was negative as well as positive interprofessional collaboration in this situation. Referring back to the principles of successful interprofessional collaborations, we will deconstruct the situation to see what went wrong.

The instructor's nursing student had been asked to administer a drug to her patient. The student approached the nursing faculty member with a problem. She had looked the drug up in the *Physician's Desk Reference* (PDR), and the prescribed dosage was four times the recommended dose. The teacher instructed the student to call and discuss this discrepancy with the pharmacy. The pharmacist confirmed that the amount exceeded the recommended dose, and risked harming the patient. The pharmacist advised the nursing student to call the physician to discuss the concern. The student was reluctant to disturb the doctor, but, recognizing her responsibility to the patient, called—with trepidation. The physician (whose own competency-based training may have set him up to respond defensively) reacted angrily, telling the student, "I am the doctor. You are the nurse. Your job is to give the medication I prescribed!" The student then returned to the instructor to seek additional counsel. The instructor reaffirmed that the student shouldn't administer the medicine. Adhering to hospital policy, the instructor and the student gave the medication to the unit nurse, who could then call the supervisor. The unit nurse empathized with the student but was similarly intimidated by the physician, and prepared to give the patient the prescribed dose.

These negative interactions could have led to a patient's receiving four times the recommended dose of a medication. Fortunately, the nursing instructor had a strong and collegial relationship with another physician. She called him and asked him to call and speak with the attending physician. A few minutes later, the unit nurses received a call from the attending physician who ordered a change in the dose to an acceptable level. The physician did not apologize for his earlier outburst, nor thank the nurses for their diligence in catching the discrepancy.

How do the Principles of Good Interprofessional Collaboration Relate to this Case Study?

Two are most relevant: (a) shared vision and (b) developing effective interpersonal and communication skills. In this case, neither the nurses on the unit nor the attending physician had established a shared vision of quality and safe patient care. However, the student nurse did see that vision in action from her instructor, the pharmacist, and the consulting physician. In a post-conference discussion, the instructor focused on the positives in the case and discussed pitfalls that prevent open and direct communications among some doctors and some nurses. To implement a shared vision, it is important to build strong relationships, establish care partnerships, and promote open and respectful two-way communication that allows all parties to effectively express their concerns affecting patient care. The instructor also discussed possible reasons why this attending physician refused to admit he was wrong, such as his training in a competitive medical education milieu (Garman et al., 2006). The faculty member suggested that the clinical manager of the unit might want to hold a workshop where the nurses could learn how to hold crucial conversations with the attending doctors. Providing opportunities for communications training for physicians would be valuable as well.

Another principle also can be seen as an outcome of effective interprofessional collaboration: developing trust and respect. In this situation, it was likely that the attending physician did not respect the input of nurses on the unit. It would be helpful for the future if the clinical manager explored this concern with the attending doctor and developed strategies to enhance trust and respect between this doctor and the hospital nursing team. The trust and respect demonstrated by the pharmacist and the consulting physician modeled a more ideal professional relationship. Educating the attending MD about the skills and expertise of the nursing team, and posting the team's nursing certifications are two options that might enhance future interactions. Hospital administrators and physician leaders also can play a role by underscoring the importance of mutual trust and respect in the healthcare setting and by promoting the expectation of professional behavior by physicians as well as other staff. A hostile work environment is not conducive to good patient care or safety.

This case is a good example of the "bad behavior" that The Joint Commission describes in its *Sentinel Event Alert* (The Joint Commission, 2008). That Alert specifically refers to "condescending language or voice intonation" (p.1 of 4), and states that this type of behavior stems from individual and systemic factors. In this instance, the nurses' fearing to speak up was symptomatic of systemic factors such as an embedded hierarchy and differences in authority. The Joint Commission's Sentinel Event Alert (2008) states that disruptive behaviors often go unaddressed for a number of reasons, including fear of retaliation and a general reluctance to confront an intimidator, thus contributing to underreporting of inappropriate behavior. The Joint Commission's new Leadership standards might have been helpful in this situation, either by preventing it or by facilitating the report of disruptive behavior.

An Example of Successful Interprofessional Collaboration

The next example is of a very successful statewide collaboration that is improving nursing education and, hopefully, patient outcomes. The Oregon Consortium of Nursing Education (OCNE, 2008), which has been discussed, includes faculty representatives from associate degree and baccalaureate nursing programs, as well as practice partners, funding agencies, and others. The Consortium's guiding principles include inclusiveness, beneficence, collegiality, courage and perseverance, healthy conflict, and shared leadership for transformation. This collaborative used all of the cited principles in developing a successful collaboration. Instead of competing with each other, faculty from the participating programs embraced a shared vision and common goals. One result was the development of a unique shared curriculum that can be utilized across programs and for multiple levels of education. This shared curriculum allows nurses with associate degrees to seamlessly enter baccalaureate programs and receive their baccalaureate degrees.

The collaboration is moving forward effectively now but did struggle to overcome some challenges. The team has shared some of their tips for a successful leadership of collaborative initiatives (personal communication: Judith Woodruff):

- Cultivate a shared vision. This is essential.
- Recruit the right mix of people, and bring the right people to the table.
- Identify an institutional warrior. This is a detailed-oriented person who will take minutes, set up meetings, and generally keep things moving.
- Prepare highlights of the expected objectives of the initiative that you can share.
- Don't waste time. Work as efficiently as possible to minimize the time burden on participants.
- Run focused and effective meetings with clear agendas.
- Identify and/or develop specific roles and tasks for the participants.
- Secure long-term commitments to minimize replacements. Otherwise, you are always "getting people up to speed."
- Be willing to add external personnel to the team if needed.

NATIONAL INITIATIVES FOR PROMOTING INTERPROFESSIONAL COLLABORATION

Barnsteiner et al. (2007) presented an excellent history of interprofessional education initiatives that have taken place in the United States. Some ongoing national programs are highlighted below:

- **ACT:** Achieving Competency Today (Ladden, Bednash, Stevens, & Moore, 2006). This program was designed as a model for interprofessional education in the areas of achieving quality, safety, and health care improvement. ACT has four modules and is an active learning program where learners from different healthcare professions design a quality improvement project. ACT is a program of Partners in Quality Education, a national initiative of The Robert Wood Johnson Foundation, USA.
- **FLIEPPS:** Faculty Leadership in Interprofessional Education to Promote Patient Safety. In a cooperative agreement with the Health Services Resource Administration (HRSA), the University of Washington's Center for Health Sciences Interprofessional Education and Research developed this national curriculum for interprofessional education to promote patient safety. Their comprehensive handbook can be downloaded from http://interprofessional.washington.edu/ptsafety/files/Handbook_Jan_05.pdf
- **QSEN:** Quality and Safety Education for Nurses (http://www.qsen.org). In this national collaborative, six competencies were identified for prelicensure registered nursing students (based on the IOM competencies), and knowledge skills and attitudes were developed for each competency. Nurse educators from around the world are sharing their best practices in teaching these competencies, via a collaborative Web site. While this national collaborative project isn't entirely about interprofessional collaboration, one of its six modules is teamwork and collaboration. Additionally, QSEN is an exemplar itself because it is a collaborative and inclusive project.
- **TeamSTEPPS.** TeamSTEPPS™ was developed by the Department of Defense (DoD) Patient Safety Program in collaboration with the Agency for Healthcare Research and Quality (AHRQ). This program is an evidence-based teamwork system aimed at optimizing patient

outcomes by improving communication and other teamwork skills among healthcare professionals. For example, one of their mutual support strategies could have been used in the student case study. The unit nurse could have used their CUS strategy, which stands for "I'm **C**oncerned," "I'm **U**ncomfortable," and "This is a **S**afety issue." This Web site has more information about training for TeamSTEPPS: http://dodpatientsafety.usuhs.mil/index.php?name=News&file=article&sid=31

DISCUSSION QUESTIONS

1. Multidisciplinary healthcare providers often work or are educated side-by-side but with little interaction between the groups. For example, prelicensure student nurses may be caring for their patients at the same time the medical interns and residents are caring for the very same patients. Yet, the nursing students communicate only with their professors and the staff nurses, while the medical students and residents communicate with their professors and attending physicians. Thinking outside the box develops strategies that would allow for more interaction between the multidisciplinary students, with the goal of fostering interprofessional collaboration in the long-term.
2. In a palliative care setting (hospice), a patient's care team includes a physician, nurse, psychologist, dietitian, chaplain, social worker, pharmacist, volunteer, and physical therapist. The team meets weekly with the patient's family. Each team member has the same goal for the patient, that is, to allow the patient experience the best quality of life possible until his or her death. Explain how this situation fosters interprofessional collaboration. What are the differences between an interprofessional collaboration in this setting, versus in a large academic medical center?
3. What do you see as the biggest barriers to interprofessional collaboration in your workplace? Using the principles described in this chapter, how can you address them?

REFERENCES

Abramson, J. S., & Mizrahi, T. (1996). When social workers and physicians collaborate: Positive and negative experiences. *Social Work, 41*, 270–281.

American Association of Colleges of Nursing. (2008). *The essentials of baccalaureate nursing education (A draft revision).* Retrieved October 12, 2008 from http://www.aacn.nche.edu/Education/pdf/BEdraft.pdf

American Association of Colleges of Nursing. (2007). *White paper on the education and role of the clinical nurse leader.* Retrieved October 12, 2008 from http://www.aacn.nche.edu/Publications/WhitePapers/ClinicalNurseLeader07.pdf

Arford, P. H. (2005). Nurse-physician communication: An organizational accountability. *Nursing Economics, 23,* 72–77.

Baggs, J. G., & Ryan, S. A. (1990). Intensive care unit nurse-physician collaboration and nurse satisfaction. *Nursing Economics, 8,* 386–392.

Barnsteiner, J. H., Disch, J. M., Hall, L., Mayer, D., & Moore, S. M. (2007). Promoting interprofessional education. *Nursing Outlook, 55,* 144–150.

Barr, H., Koppel, I., Reeves, S., Hammick, M., & Freeth, D. (2005). *Effective interprofessional education: Argument, assumption & evidence.* Oxford, UK: Blackwell Publishing.

Boswell, C., & Cannon, S. (January 31, 2005). New horizons for collaborative partnerships. *Online Journal of Issues in Nursing, 10.* Retrieved May 30, 2008 from http://www.medscape.com/viewarticle/499267

Coeling, H. V., & Wilcox, J. R. (1994). Steps to collaboration. *Nursing Administration Quarterly, 18,* 44–55.

Cullen, L., Fraser, D., & Symonds, I. (2003). Strategies for interprofessional education: The interprofessional team objective structured clinical examination for midwifery and medical students. *Nurse Education Today, 23,* 427–433.

Erickson, B., McHarney-Brown, C., Seeger, K., & Kaufman, A. (July 1998). Overcoming barriers to interprofessional health sciences education. *Education for Health: Change in Learning & Practice, 11,* 143–149.

Gardner, D. B. (January 31, 2005). Ten lessons in collaboration. *Online Journal of Issues in Nursing, 10.* Retrieved July 1, 2008 from http://www.medscape.com/viewarticle/499266

Garman, A. N., Leach, D. C., & Spector, N. (2006). Worldviews in collision: Conflict and collaboration across professional lines. *Journal of Organizational Behavior, 27,* 829–849.

Glen, S. (2004). Interprofessional education: The evidence base influencing policy and policy makers. *Nurse Education Today, 24,* 157–159.

Glen, S., & Reeves, S. (2004). Developing interprofessional education in pre-registration curricula: mission impossible? *Nurse Education in Practice, 4,* 45–52.

Greiner, A. C., & Knebel, E. (Eds.) (2003). *Health Professions Education: A Bridge to Quality.* Washington DC: National Academies Press.

Hader, R. (2008) Workplace violence: Survey 2008. *Nursing Management,* 39(7), 13–19.

Institute of Medicine. (2001). *Crossing the Quality Chasm: A New Health System for the 21st Century.* Washington D.C.: National Academies Press.

Knaus, W. A., Draper, E. A., Wagner, D. P., & Zimmerman, J. E. (1986). Evaluation of outcomes from intensive care in major medical centers. *Annals of Internal Medicine,* 104, 410–418.

Kohn, L. T., Corrigan, J. M., & Donaldson, M. S. (Eds.) (2000). *To Err is Human: Building a Safer Health System*. Washington, DC: National Academies Press.

Ladden, M. D., Bednash, G., Stevens, D. P., & Moore, G. T. (2006). Educating interprofessional learners for quality, safety and systems improvement. *Journal of Interprofessional Care, 20*, 497–505.

Lindeke, L., & Sieckert, A. (January 31, 2005). Nurse-physician workplace collaboration. *Online Journal of Issues in Nursing*, 10(1). Retrieved July 1, 2008 from http://www.nursingworld.org/mods/mod775/nrsdrfull.htm

McCool, W. F. (2004). On competition and collaboration: Nursing, midwifery, and *U.S. News & World Report. Journal of Professional Nursing, 20*, 143–144.

MacKay, S. (2004). The role perception questionnaire (RPQ): A tool for assessing undergraduate students' perceptions of the role of other professions. *Journal of Interprofessional Care, 18*, 289–302.

McKay, C. A., & Crippen, L. (2008), Collaboration through clinical integration. *Nursing Administration Quarterly, 32*, 109–116.

Mendez, M. J. P., Armayor, N. C., Navarlaz, M. T. D., & Wakefield, A. (2008). The potential advantages and disadvantages of introducing interprofessional education into the healthcare curricula in Spain. *Nurse Education Today, 28*, 327–336.

National Council of State Boards of Nursing. (2004). *Model nursing practice act and rules*. Retrieved October 12, 2008 from https://www.ncsbn.org/312.htm

National Council of State Boards of Nursing. (2006). *National study of elements of nursing education*. Retrieved October 12, 2008 from https://www.ncsbn.org/Vol_24_web.pdf

National League for Nursing Accrediting Commission. (2008). *Standards and criteria*. Retrieved October 12, 2008 from http://www.nlnac.org/manuals/SC2008.htm

Oregon Consortium of Nursing Education (OCNE). (2008). *Guiding principles and norms for OCNE Coordinating Council and staff*. Retrieved October 12, 2008 from http://www.ocne.org/guiding_principles.html

O'Halloran, C., Hean, S., Humphris, D., & MacLeod-Clark. (2006). Developing common learning: The New Generation Project undergraduate curriculum model, *Journal of Interprofessional Care, 20*, 12–28.

Oxford English Dictionary. Retrieved April 30, 2008 from http://www.oed.com

Reeves, S., Freeth, D., Glen, S., Lieba, T., Berridge, E. J., & Herzberg, J. (2006). Delivering practice-based interprofessional education to community mental health teams: Understanding some key lessons. *Nurse Education in Practice, 6*, 246–253.

Schmalenberg, C., Kramer, M., King, C. R., & Krugman, M. (2005). Securing collegial/collaborative nurse-physician relationships, part I. *The Journal of Nursing Administration, 35*, 450–458.

Silver, M. P. & Antonow, J. A. (2000). Reducing medication errors in hospitals: A peer review organization collaboration. *Joint Commission Journal on Quality Improvement, 26*, 332–340.

Steinert, Y. (May 2005). Learning together to teach together: Interprofessional education and faculty development. *Journal of Interprofessional Care, Supplement 1:* 60–75.

Stone (2006). Evaluating interprofessional education: The tautological need for interdisciplinary approaches. *Journal of Interprofessional Care*, 20(3), 260–275.

The Cochrane Collaboration. (2008). Retrieved October 12, 2008 from http://www.cochrane.org/

The Joint Commmission. (2008). *Sentinel Event Alert: Behaviors that undermine a culture of safety*. Retrieved on Accessed October 12, 2008 from http://www.jointcommission.org/NewsRoom/NewsReleases/nr_07_09_08.htm

Walsh, C. L., Gordon, M. F., Marshall, M., Wilson, F., & Hunt, T. (2005). Interprofessional capability: A developing framework for interprofessional education. *Nurse Education in Practice, 5*, 230–237.

Weeks, W. B., Mills, P. D., Dittus, R. S., Dittus, D. C., & Batalden, P. B. (2001). Using an improvement model to reduce adverse drug events in VA facilities. *Joint Commission Journal on Quality Improvement, 27*, 640–646.

Wolff, T. & Associates. (Summer 2005). *Collaborative Solutions Newsletter*. Retrieved October 12, 2008 from http://www.tomwolff.com/collaborative-solutions-newsletter-summer-05.htm

Zarenstein, M., & Bryant, W. (2000). Interventions to promote collaboration between doctors and nurses. *Cochrane Database of Systematic Reviews*, Issue 2. Art. No.: CD000072. DO1: 10.1002/14651858.CD000072.

Zarenstein, M., Reeves, S., Barr, H., Hammick, M., Koppel, I., & Atkins, J. (2000). Interprofessional education: Effects on professional practice and health care outcomes. *Cochrane Database of Systematic Reviews*, Issue 3. Art. No. D002213.DO13. DOI:10.1002/14651858. CD002213.

CHAPTER 6

Management and Administration of Collaborative Models

Joni Novosel, MSHA; Ronald Sorensen, MSHA

LEARNING OBJECTIVES

After completing this chapter, the reader should be able to:

1. Describe the benefits of collaboration in the healthcare field.
2. Understand the best approaches for promoting success of a collaborative team or project.
3. Discuss some of the challenges of managing a collaborative team and how to overcome those challenges.
4. Assess the readiness of the organization and team to collaborate.
5. Develop insight on the best processes for developing a collaborative model in the healthcare field.
6. Identify the different tools that can be used to help develop a collaborative team or project in a healthcare setting.
7. Discuss some of the best practices in collaboration within the healthcare industry.

KEY TERMS

Advocacy
Aligned
Coalitions
Collective partnerships
Consensus
Facilitator
Initiatives
Interdisciplinary collaboration
Likert Scale
Readiness assessment
Stakeholders

INTRODUCTION

Importance of Collaboration in the Health Care Setting and How to Ensure Success

Collaboration, specifically the cooperation between agencies that are not immediately connected, is critical in today's society within and among hospitals, clinics, community-based organizations, mental health providers, alcohol and substance abuse providers, and nonprofit agencies. Private and public healthcare organizations, for example, increasingly need to rely on each other, given the complicated interdependencies involved in serving an entire community. The blurring of lines between individual and population-based health is forcing practitioners to become adept at understanding and functioning effectively and collaboratively in both private and public worlds (Mitchell & Crittenden, 2000).

Realistically, community problems are complex and necessitate comprehensive solutions. Many of these solutions fall outside the realm of what one agency alone can accomplish, and require the participation of professionals with diverse backgrounds and expertise to address the issues and social needs faced by clients and consumers. For example, from a management perspective, the problem of lack of continuity of care can be addressed through interdisciplinary collaboration and collective partnerships that provide a seamless coordination of care to patients. The result: improved community health outcomes. These types of collaborations have been demonstrated to be an effective tool in health care and are important to the future health and well-being of the community.

As the cost of provision of healthcare services soars, collaborations and partnerships become important to most effectively use finite resources in the healthcare field. Available funding streams are limited today, with many needy agencies competing for scarce dollars. To best harness the dollars available to achieve improved outcomes, it is wiser to seek out collaborative solutions instead of using a silo approach, which may duplicate services and result in unnecessary costs.

Additionally, there is strength in numbers; a group that broadens its base and involves more contributing stakeholders is more likely to be successful in its goals (Robinson, 2004). To that end, federal, state, and local requests for proposals and foundation grants are identifying collaboration as a requirement to receive funds. Statewide and geographically-based projects, for example, expect coalitions to be representative of key stakeholders who will provide a broad range of coordinated healthcare services to their community's vulnerable populations. Some grant providers are valuing collaboration for resolution of integrated issues when making funding decisions, and may even provide a template that outlines which participants should be included in a coalition to promote the best outcomes. Foundations can maximize the use of their grant resources when projects and programs are working in collaborations that are effective and sustainable, and many foundations are particularly intrigued by joint projects involving new and existing collaborators (Robinson, 2004). Fostering a collaborative environment has become a critical component of project success.

Most professionals engaging in collaborative endeavors continue to work within their own organization while, at the same time, transcending the boundaries of that setting to link up with professionals and organizations in other organizations or sectors. Effective collaboration includes implemented strategies that enable professionals and organizations from different "cultures" to work together in a common enterprise towards a common goal (Lasker & Committee, 1997). As each agency brings its own unique culture and agenda to the collaboration, it can be easy for the group to lose the focus on its goal and revert to individual agency priorities unless there is strong leadership of the coalition or collaborative. Participants in a successful coalition or collaboration should know their specific roles and work toward a clear objective with a shared sense of commitment (Robinson, 2004).

As professionals attempting to help our communities to achieve better health, now and in the future, we have to collaborate to survive (Mitchell & Crittenden, 2000). In addition to promoting individual agencies' endeavors to make a positive impact on the continuum of care for patients, the most important reason to be part of a coalition is the greater potential for public outreach. Many grassroots organizations struggle to have their voice heard beyond their own membership ranks. For these groups, collaborative projects can move their message onto a broader public stage, where it can be heard, perhaps for the first time, from familiar and trustworthy sources (Robinson, 2004). Organizations looking to expand the reach of providers' impact on the community or simply trying to maintain the high level of quality care in today's cost-conscious environment have discovered that collaboration is a key enabler for success in the healthcare industry.

BENEFITS OF COLLABORATION

Leaders of collaborative teams should ensure that the participants at the table understand the benefits and value of collaborating. Collaboration takes time and effort. Members of the group need to understand why these efforts are necessary to achieve the true benefits of collaboration. The following lists some of the key benefits of collaboration that leaders should communicate.

Better Outcomes for the Patient or Client

A recent study conducted at 14 hospitals with a "magnet" designation from the American Nurses Credentialing Center, demonstrated that healthy collaborative relationships between physicians and nurses were not only possible, but were directly linked to optimal patient outcomes (Kramer & Schmalenberg, 2003). When people are working together and feel like they are part of a team with a shared purpose, then professionalism is enhanced, trust among group members is increased, communication flows better, and satisfaction of those on the team is increased.

Improved Efficiency of Operations

If collaboration is successful, then efficiency in the use of staff and other resources is improved. The equation for truly effective collaboration in a group is 1 + 1 = 3, meaning that the outcome or end result of each contribution to the collaboration is *more* than the sum of its parts. As stated by Thomas Backer of the Human Interaction Institute, "It is important to look at the costs and benefits of collaborating over the long haul, including evaluation when appropriate" (Backer, 2007). The benefits of improved efficiency through collaboration come from tapping into the unique perspectives, ideas, and resources that each member of the collaborative team brings to the table to address a particular issue. Through collaboration, the duplication of resources or individual efforts can be reduced or eliminated. However, if collaboration is slowing an organization's progress towards its goals or exacting too high a cost, then a cost/benefit analysis should be done to determine if the benefits of collaborating outweigh the costs involved.

Generating New Ideas or Approaches to Address Issues and Problems

Bringing a group of individuals from different disciplines, personalities, and backgrounds together in a collaborative process can inspire the generation of new and unique ideas and solutions to address problems and issues. Collaboration involves an exchange of views and ideas that reflect the perspectives of all the collaborators, whether or not agreement is reached in the interaction (Coeling & Cukr, 1997). With different disciplines and/or viewpoints at the table, an expectation of mutual respect by and towards all participants is critical to the collaboration's success. All ideas and input should be heard and given fair consideration by the group.

Increased Employee and Client Satisfaction

Professionalism among the members of a collaborative group is strengthened if participants believe that their ideas are being heard, and that a diversity of opinion and expertise is welcomed in the quest to achieve the common goal. Contributors want to be part of the group because they see the positive outcomes and benefits of participation. Active leadership and facilitation of the group and acknowledgment of the group's accomplishments promote group progress and success. Groups that do not treat participants with respect or value their ideas and contributions will see a high attrition rate and/or poorer outcomes.

Collaborative partnerships are worth the investment because they produce improved healthcare outcomes for patients and clients as well as promote professional development for participants (Kramer & Schmalenberg, 2003).

CHALLENGES OF MANAGING A COLLABORATIVE MODEL

The benefits of collaboration usually outweigh the challenges. Leaders of coalitions, however, should be prepared to face and overcome some common challenges to the collaborative process.

Individual Resistance to Working Together

Personal conflicts, strong or domineering personalities, resistance to change, and pessimistic attitudes are a few of the roadblocks that can undermine effective collaboration. Participants may be negatively influenced by unproductive or challenging experiences in their past (Backer, 2007). Overcoming this resistance requires skill and persistence by the person facilitating or directing the collaborative team.

Bringing People from Different Disciplines Together to Work on a Project

One of the key challenges for healthcare collaborations is the effective integration of a diverse group of participants who are trained in different disciplines and often use language unique to their field. In addition to the diversity of culture, religion, ethnicity, etc. that is seen in today's healthcare workplace, healthcare professionals today come from diverse fields such as nursing and medicine, which have been strongly influenced by the philosophies and content of their educational programs, by the unique jargon of each discipline, and by professional cultural norms (Lindeke & Block, 1998). The potential for individual conflict and resistance is not insignificant. For example, in a collaborative team providing patient care, a nurse may try to develop a consensus among the team for a patient treatment plan, while the physician may be focusing on ruling out alternatives and identifying a primary diagnosis. Both disciplines bring value to the team, but the potential for conflict exists if the team members are unable to comprehend and respect the others' perspectives and positive contributions to the final outcomes.

Time Commitment Needed in Developing a Collaborative Model

As mentioned previously, collaboration takes time and effort for those involved in the process. Clear expectations as to the time commitment needed should be relayed to the group members at the start of a project. Supervisors should approve release time for participants because without management support, staff may not be able to commit the necessary time to the team. Unfortunately, collaborative initiatives can sometimes be a tactic for delaying action or obscuring responsibility with the result that change is obstructed (Backer, 2007). Additionally, if group members do not see positive progress from an initiative, or their role is not well-defined, they may be less inclined to invest needed time and effort in a project.

Ensuring that Everyone Contributes to the Process

For collaboration to be successful, every participant must be willing to contribute and offer his or her knowledge, insight, and perspective. Group projects where only a few people contribute are not really collaborative. A team leader needs to be wary of participants with strong personalities who try to dominate the discussion or gain power within the group. Typically, Type A personalities are rewarded for their driven, competitive approach (Kai & Drinkwater, 2004). But, subversively trying to gain power within the group can be detrimental to the process and may lead to an outcome that was unplanned or not in line with the project's goals. Dealing with dominating individuals requires effective communication skills to guide and channel the participant's behavior and promote cooperation among the group. At the other end of the spectrum, dealing with the quiet individual also takes skill. Sometimes people can be timid about contributing to the team for fear that their ideas will not be taken seriously or might be viewed unfavorably by the rest of the group. The group leader should create a "comfort zone" for these individuals by relaying that all ideas will be heard and treated with respect, and that contribution is an expectation for everyone. Positive reinforcement also works well in these situations; contributors are praised and complimented for their ideas and input.

Overseeing the Process and Keeping it On Track

Another challenge for a group leader is to keep the collaborators moving forward with their eyes on the goal. Focusing on the expected outcome of a collaboration is easier if clearly stated goals and objectives have been presented to the team at the start of the project. A skilled leader then should be able to provide direction to the group when challenges arise. In some cases, an external facilitator may need to be brought in to help guide the group through the process towards the goals. Investing the resources in an experienced consultant to assist the group may result in improved progress and outcomes that effectively "recoups" the cost.

In sum, a good team leader should be able to build a solid team, negotiate collaborative relationships respectfully, manage conflict wisely, discourage and prevent negative behaviors within the group, communicate skillfully, put out "fires," and create an environment that promotes collaboration (Vickers, 2007). Finally, the outstanding leader is able to analyze and learn from what goes wrong as well as from what goes right. The lessons and skills learned from a less-than-ideal collaboration might help the insightful leader improve the next collaboration he or she helms.

ASSESSING THE READINESS OF THE ORGANIZATION AND TEAM TO COLLABORATE

As already noted, one of a team leader's first tasks is to assess if the team is ready to collaborate. Not all problems can be solved by collaboration; sometimes the right decision is *not* to collaborate (Backer, 2007). Conducting a readiness assessment with the proposed team can evaluate organization, team, and participant preparedness for collaboration. Two examples of such readiness assessment tools follows.

Colorado Department of Public Health and Environment

The Tony Grampsas Youth Services (TGYS) Grant administered through the Colorado Department of Public Health and Environment offers a good collaboration assessment tool. The assessment looks at six dimensions of collaboration (TGYS, 2007).

- *Collaboration Membership:* To what extent do the members of the collaborative team have a strong commitment to the collaboration?
- *Collaboration Structure:* To what extent does the collaboration have effective norms, rules, support, facilities, etc.?
- *Collaboration Leadership:* To what extent does the collaborative team have strong, knowledgeable, and engaged leaders?
- *Internal Collaboration:* To what extent do members within the collaborative team effectively work together?
- *Collaboration Effectiveness:* To what extent has the collaborative team set specific measurable goals and achieved them?

- *Collaboration Sustainability:* To what extent has your collaborative team worked toward and achieved long term sustainability plans?

A series of questions are asked for each of the above dimensions. Members of the team are asked to score the questions on a scale of 1 to 9 (1 = very strongly disagree; 9 = very strongly agree), and the scores are then averaged to identify areas of team strength and opportunities for improvement.

- *Collaboration Membership Considerations:*
  - Members are willing to devote whatever effort is necessary to achieve common goals.
  - Members monitor the effectiveness of the process (they look at what is working and continue doing it and make changes to what is not working).
  - The diversity of each partner agency (or team member) is valued and reflected in this collaboration.
  - Members of my collaboration are committed to the collaboration.
  - I enjoy being a member of this multi-agency (or multidiscipline) collaboration.
- *Collaboration Structure Considerations:*
  - Members have agreed on how decisions will be made by the group.
  - We have a method for communicating the activities and decisions of the group to all members (e.g., listservs, e-mails, minutes, etc.).
  - Our collaborative is willing to talk about and improve the way we do things when different processes or approaches aren't working.
  - There are clearly defined roles and responsibilities for collaborative team members.
- *Collaboration Leadership Considerations:*
  - The multi-agency or multidisciplinary collaboration has effective leadership.
  - The collaboration leaders are able to continually energize the members.
  - The collaboration leaders are able to mobilize members toward common goals.
  - The collaboration leaders make me feel welcome at meetings.
  - The collaboration leaders understand the values and culture of each team member.
- *Internal Collaboration Considerations:*
  - We frequently discuss how we are working together.

  - We celebrate our group's successes as we move forward toward achieving the final goal.
  - My collaboration is effective in resolving conflict within the group.
  - Members trust each other sufficiently to honestly and accurately share information, perceptions, and feedback.
- *Collaboration Effectiveness Considerations:*
  - As a result of this collaboration, services/programs to address the needs of the client, community, or patient have improved.
  - As a result of this collaboration, accessibility to services and programs has improved.
  - As a result of this collaboration, policies, rules, or laws have been changed to support a new, effective way of "doing business."
  - As a result of this collaboration, people are better off in our organization/community/department.
- *Collaboration Sustainability Considerations:*
  - The organizers stay with the effort even through the hard times to help the collaborative team overcome obstacles.
  - The collaboration has kept the demands on members simple and realistic.
  - The collaboration does not rely too heavily on any one member.
  - The collaboration has explored ways of sustaining its efforts (e.g., financial support, commitment of staff time, etc.).
- *Other Questions to Consider:*
  - What recommendations do you have for improving this collaboration?
  - What do you think is working well in this collaboration?

Key Areas for the Team to Assess

The assessment developed by the Colorado Department of Public Health and Environment for the TGYS Program is an example of a good in-depth approach to evaluating whether a collaborative team will be successful. For those collaborative teams seeking a shorter assessment tool, the key questions below, with open-ended responses or a Likert scale, could be considered at a project's start.

- Does this project or issue lend itself to a collaborative approach?
- Do you have the right leadership to oversee the collaborative team?
- Is everyone willing to give of their time to collaborate on the project?

- Do the team members understand what collaboration means?
- Are people willing to put aside their competitive/professional/other differences for the good of the collaboration?
- Can the benefits of collaboration be clearly identified for this project or issue or problem?
- Do the benefits outweigh the drawbacks for collaborating?
- Does the organization's leadership value collaboration and support the work of the team?

The responses to these questions, based on key readiness and success indicators, will allow the team and its leaders to assess its readiness to collaborate and its potential chances of success (see Figure 6-1).

Process for Developing a Collaborative Model

In the current environment of economic pressures, resource limitations, and demands for accountability, professionals and community-based organizations in health care clearly need each other to successfully achieve their missions and meet performance standards. Individuals and organizations that had functioned historically in silos are now encouraged and guided to form relationships across sectors. This transition may not always proceed smoothly. Common stumbling blocks are highlighted by the following questions: Are professionals and organizations in sectors that have grown foreign to each other able to identify their mutual interests? Are they able to overcome their concerns and skepticism adequately enough to initiate a

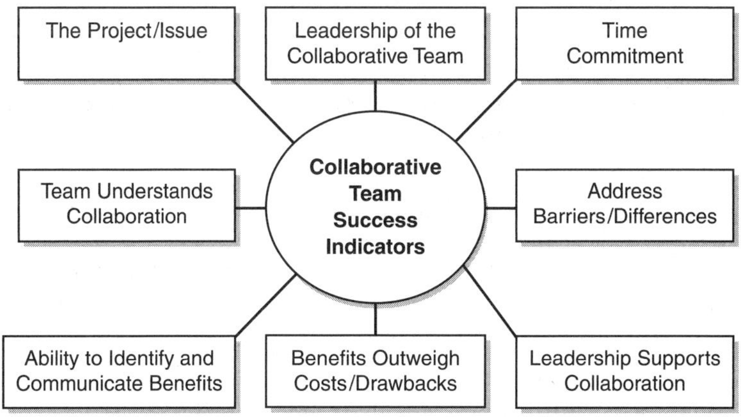

FIGURE 6-1. Assessment of a Team's Readiness to Collaborate

working relationship? Are they able to identify potential partners and forecast how their resources and skills can be harnessed in a collaborative endeavor? (Lasker & Committee, 1997)

Obviously, the management and administration of a collaborative approach to a problem is not a simple process. Managers and administrators should specifically seek out partners who are willing to work jointly and work with agencies that possess a culture of cooperation. Those managers and administrators who undervalue collaborative approaches may not reach optimal project outcomes if they continue to function in traditional silos.

Ensure Everyone Is Clear on the Reason(s) for Collaborating

As stated previously, a very important step in the process for the collaborative leader is to make certain that everyone understands the reason for collaborating. Each of the partners needs to agree and value the project.

Communicate a Clear Vision and End Point

The vision and goals of the project must be communicated and understood by the group also. A collaborative leader can build his or her own communication skills even while assisting team members with theirs. Effective communication requires that all team participants possess active listening skills and are able to relay messages in a clear and concise manner. Many times, a consultant is brought in as an unbiased or neutral facilitator to help team members communicate more effectively, diplomatically, and productively. Good channels of communication help build a common language among partners; foster trust and mutual respect; support group decision-making; keep partners fully informed about coalition progress; enable partners to learn about each others' concerns, values, work, and disagreements; and provide them with avenues to respond to changes and emerging problems (Lasker & Committee, 1997).

Clarify Individual Team Members' Roles and Responsibilities

Another role of the collaborative leader is to advise the group what the expectations of each team member will be. This can be accomplished by creating and sharing with each member clearly defined roles and responsibilities, that is, how the work will be done and who will do it. A clearly defined work plan with feasible timelines will help the process flow more smoothly.

Develop an Environment That Encourages Participation

A collaborative leader should create a culture of collaboration and promote an environment that encourages participation by all members of the team. Factors that influence broad participation include the location of the meeting(s); the size and set-up of the meeting area; the encouragement of open dialogue, trust, and respect; a clearly defined decision making process; and timely and effective conflict resolution.

Tools for Developing a Collaborative Approach

With increased demands for collaborative approaches, many books and Web sites offer resources to assist healthcare organizations with tools to develop their own successful collaborations and coalitions. The Prevention Institute has developed an extremely valuable Eight-Step Process for building a successful collaboration.

The Prevention Institute's Model for Collaboration

Founded in 1997, The Prevention Institute is a nonprofit, national center, dedicated to improving community health and well-being by building

Table 6-1. The Prevention Institute's Eight Steps to Building an Effective Coalition

Step	Description
Step1	Analyze the program's objectives and determine whether to form a coalition
Step 2	Recruit the right people
Step 3	Devise a set of preliminary objectives and activities
Step 4	Convene the coalition
Step 5	Anticipate the necessary resources
Step 6	Define elements of a successful coalition structure
Step 7	Maintain coalition vitality
Step 8	Make improvements through evaluation

Source: Adapted from The Prevention Institute.

momentum for programs promoting effective primary prevention. Its model, "Developing Effective Coalitions: An Eight Step Guide," was originally developed at the Contra Costa County (California) Health Services Department Prevention Program to assist public health organizations in developing effective community coalitions to prevent injuries (Cohen, Baer, & Satterwhite, 2002).

Step 1. Analyze the program's objectives and determine whether to form a coalition. It is important to determine if a collaborative approach to a problem is the best one. The Prevention Institute suggests the following three steps to determine if a coalition should be developed:

1. Clarify the objectives and appropriate activities. (What needs to be done?)
2. Assess community strengths and weaknesses.
3. Determine the costs and benefits to the lead agency.

In many cases, a collaborative is formed in response to a health care or social needs crisis or problem. These groups identify a common goal and shared vision such as improving air and water quality in their neighborhoods, reducing youth violence and gang activity, promoting high school graduation rates, or providing preventive low-cost health and mental heath services.

> ". . . Americans are a peculiar people . . . If, in a local community, a citizen becomes aware of a human need that is not met, he thereupon discusses the situation with his neighbors. Suddenly a committee comes into existence. The committee thereupon begins to operate on behalf of the need, and a new community function is established. It is like watching a miracle."
>
> —ALEXIS DE TOCQUEVILLE, *DEMOCRACY IN AMERICA*

Step 2. Recruit the right people. To be effective, a coalition has to have the right contributors at the table. It is important to identify which organizations, individual members, competitors, and adversaries the group should include. Once an organization has been identified, its representative should be selected. Ideally, the representative chosen should be in a decision-making position and be committed to the project. The size of the group also should fit the task of the group (Cohen et al., 2002).

In her book *Coalitions and Partners in Community Health*, Frances Butterfoss (2007) identified four recruitment approaches to assemble coalition membership: self-interest, transactional, altruistic, and social needs.

Step 3. Devise a set of preliminary objectives and activities. In Step 1, the lead agency's objectives are examined. These objectives should be aligned with the goals of the other members of the collaborative. It is important to develop goals and objectives as well as group activities that reflect the needs, mission, interests, strengths, and diversity of the coalition. Helpful steps in launching a collaboration include the early identification of a common goal, the establishment of short-term outcomes, and the avoidance of competition for funding by similar individual projects (Cohen et al., 2002).

Step 4. Convene the coalition. There are three ways that coalitions are typically initiated: 1) through a meeting; 2) at a conference; or 3) at a workshop. Meeting location and time should be convenient to maximize desired attendance. The lead agency should be well prepared with an agenda, mission, and recommendations for the coalition structure, goals, and activities. Broad-based coalitions are very effective, but leaders should understand that not all invitees may find that a particular coalition is a good fit (Cohen et al., 2002).

Step 5. Anticipate the necessary resources. It is important for coalition leaders to develop budgets and map agency resources and needs. Substantial time commitments are required of the lead agency as well as the ability to provide staffing and funding support as needed to keep the coalition viable and functioning. It is important to recognize that coalition members' time is their most valuable contribution to the group, and should be used wisely (Cohen et al., 2002).

Step 6. Define elements of a successful coalition structure. It is important to devise a solid framework for the coalition. Structural issues to consider are: a) coalition life expectancy; b) meeting location, frequency, and length; c) membership parameters; d) the decision-making process; e) meeting agendas; and f) expectations and logistics for participation between meetings (Cohen et al., 2002).

Step 7. Maintain coalition vitality. Leadership of a coalition needs to promote the coalition's vitality and renewal. This can be accomplished through developing and implementing methods for identifying and addressing problems, sharing power and leadership, recruiting and involving new members, providing training, bringing challenging new issues to the group, and celebrating and sharing successes. It is important for leaders to recognize both individual and organizational contributions (Cohen et al., 2002).

Step 8. Make improvements through evaluation. Evaluations can provide important feedback to the coalition. When assessments are performed throughout a project cycle, they provide the team with data that can guide improvements. Meaningful evaluation should increase the effectiveness of the coalition process as well as enhance the outcomes of the coalition's work (Cohen et al., 2002).

The model was used in forming the collaborative and continues to be used as the basis for new coalitions. The Diabetes Collaborative will be discussed later in this chapter as a case study.

BEST PRACTICES

There are many best practices among collaboration efforts within the healthcare industry. This chapter focuses on two: the Los Angeles County's Public-Private Partnership Model and the U.S. national anti-smoking initiatives.

Los Angeles County Public-Private Partnership Model

In 1995, a financial crisis was facing the Los Angeles County Department of Health Services (LADHS). Faced with a huge deficit, the Department was considering closing facilities, reducing services, and limiting access. Up until this point in time, the Department of Health Services had been focused mostly on its hospital operations with less attention paid to clinic services. County clinic services had been fully funded from the County budget and were publicly owned.

In response to the fiscal crisis, the County met with representatives from the Federal Government, and was able to negotiate an 1115 waiver under the Medicaid program to bring additional funding to the LADHS. One stipulation of this augmented funding, however, was that outpatient capacity (clinic services) had to be increased. Because the LADHS operated a limited number of clinics, they invited private clinics to the table to develop a partnership that would help the County expand capacity as required.

As a result, the Public Private Partnership (PPP) Program was launched. Its main goal was to increase outpatient capacity for uninsured individuals residing in Los Angeles County. Since its inception, the program has evolved into a best practice model of collaboration between a public entity and private providers in the community, and has benefited all the partners involved in the project. LADHS was able to meet the requirements of the Federal waiver and the private clinics were provided Federal funding to help care for the additional uninsured patients. Most importantly, patients benefited through the expanded access to medical care.

The PPP Program continues today and has reported some positive outcomes that are helpful guides for collaboration:

- Partners were clear regarding their roles and responsibilities in the program.
- Contractual agreements were signed between the County and the private clinics, establishing a formal relationship among the parties.
- By bringing the appropriate parties to the table and coordinating the cost-effective use of resources, health services capacity was expanded, resulting in improved access to primary care.
- Improved cost-efficiency resulted from this collaboration. The private clinics were able to treat patients at a lower cost per visit then the County clinics.
- Systems were improved to create a more seamless movement of patients between the private sector and County providers. These systems were the result of joint brainstorming among the collaborative partners in the PPP Program.

U.S. National Anti-Smoking Coalitions

In 1950, works by the German-born American physician Ernst L. Wynder, and by the British statisticians Austin Bradford Hill and Sir Richard Doll, provided firm evidence linking lung cancer with smoking. This information came as a considerable shock to smokers, who proved reluctant to give up their cigarettes. Even after reports were released from the Royal College of Physicians (1962) and the U.S. Surgeon General (1964) clearly stating the deleterious health effects of smoking, quit rates were not as high as might have been expected. In the 1950s and early 1960s, anti-smoking organizations were addressing the issue from their own silos, and their efforts were not as effective as subsequent collaborative initiatives. Recent successes are a result of the collaboration of many health associations and concerned groups to educate the public about the dangers of smoking.

In the 1970s and 1980s agencies began to address the issue collaboratively on a larger scale. The American Lung Association (ALA), American Thoracic Society, and the Congress of Lung Association Staff started the Collaborative Smoking Cessation Project. U.S. Surgeon General C. Everett Koop also selected representatives from 23 agencies to create an expert tobacco control panel.

In 1997, the ALA formed a new tobacco-control advocacy group under the slogan "Save Lives, Not Tobacco": The Coalition for Accountability, a coalition of over 350 public health, consumer, medical, civic, labor, and business groups advocating fair and effective tobacco-control policies at local, state, and national levels.

Positive outcomes from their collaborative approaches include:

- Warning labels on cigarette packaging
- Broadcast advertising bans
- Smoking ban on all interstate buses and domestic airline flights
- Smoke-free restaurants and bars
- Smoke-free workplaces
- Smoke-free cities
- Successful lawsuits against tobacco companies
- Smoking in the United States has dropped from 30% to under 20% in the last 20 years

CASE STUDIES

The following case studies are examples of successful collaborative projects and programs in a nonprofit coalition or consortium setting. Established in 1995, Valley Care Community Consortium (VCCC) is a nonprofit health and mental health planning collaborative working in Service Planning Area 2 (SPA 2) of Los Angeles County. "VCCC creates healthier communities in the San Fernando and Santa Clarita Valleys through collaboration, partnership, and implementation of innovative programs, with emphasis on vulnerable populations." VCCC has a diverse membership that has grown from 10 community stakeholder and safety net providers in 1995, to 265 in 2007, and has remained at the forefront of collaborative community efforts to identify as well as reduce health disparities. For over a decade, VCCC founders and members have realized the importance of collaboration to effect positive change. VCCC is uniquely qualified to engage, mobilize, and lead coalitions of community stakeholders through the process of developing and implementing a collaborative plan of action.

Triennial Community Needs Assessment

In November 1996, a group of hospitals in the San Fernando and Santa Clarita Valleys began a dialogue regarding working together on a joint health needs assessment of the area. Legislation passed in the State of California had mandated that nonprofit hospitals conduct a community needs assessment every three years. The hospitals realized that it made sense to do a joint assessment, instead of each hospital having to take on its own project. Because VCCC was already functioning collaboratively in the area, the hospitals agreed to partner with VCCC on this project. Pooling resources, staff, and expertise from the hospitals together with VCCC resources resulted in a more comprehensive and complete study of the area.

Since 1997, the group of organizations participating in the community needs assessment has grown. In 2007, the fourth consecutive collaborative assessment was completed, with over 37 organizations actively participating in the project and contributing staff, resources, and leadership support. The commitment of the participating organizations to this collaborative project is due in large part to the benefits, such as valuable data, that the organizations receive from being part of this effort.

Pacoima Diabetes/Obesity Prevention and Management Project

In late 2004, as a result of the VCCC 2004 Triennial Community Needs Assessment, VCCC engaged partners to form a Chronic Disease subcommittee. A major task of the subcommittee was to create a collaborative project that would include agencies with the skill sets and resources to carry out the goal of reducing obesity and diabetes within a collaborative framework.

The subcommittee developed eight objectives to address this goal and determined that the project needed to consist of seven different partners in addition to VCCC. Leaders from these seven participating agencies would form a smaller subcommittee known as the Pacoima Diabetes Collaborative, which acted as a steering committee for the project.

Funding provided by the California Endowment supported this collaborative in its goal to increase access to a coordinated and comprehensive system of diabetes and obesity care in Pacoima and the surrounding Northeast San Fernando Valley areas. Throughout 2005, the Pacoima Diabetes Collaborative met to develop a program that would enhance Mission

Community Hospital Project ALTO, and improve chronic disease management, provision of health benefit screenings, launch walking groups, and increase access to affordable fruits and vegetables for the target population.

For each of the eight project objectives, the steering committee members reviewed what needed to be accomplished, and assigned roles and responsibilities for each task based on the skill set and expertise of the collaborative participants. A facilitator was hired through the lead agency to help the group create a list of important points, summarize issues, share ideas, raise questions to bring out different viewpoints, guide (but not lead) the discussion, and restate ideas when needed.

The Pacoima Diabetes/Obesity Prevention and Management Project is an example of a collaborative community-based approach to provide prevention and education to an underserved population. As our communities struggle to meet the health requirements of our population with limited fiscal and human resources, collaboration will be the key to successfully providing needed health care and education services across our nation.

CONCLUSION

> *"None of us is as smart as all of us . . . . We all know that cooperation and collaboration grow more important every day. A shrinking world in which technological and political complexity increase at an accelerating rate offers fewer and fewer arenas in which individual action suffices."*
>
> —WARREN BENNIS, *1996*

DISCUSSION QUESTIONS

1. Why is it important for management to know when to collaborate and when to take a silo approach? Assuming you were the manager or administrator, when would you advocate for a collaborative approach? When would a silo approach work better?
2. What are some of the key challenges to managing a collaborative workgroup?
3. Discuss the different approaches that can be used to assess if a team is ready to collaborate?

4. What are some steps a manager or administrator can take to foster a climate of collaboration?

REFERENCES

Backer, T. G. (2007). *What science and common sense say about collaboration and sustainability*. Lecture, October 23.

Butterfoss, F. D., (2007). Coalitions and partnerships in community health. San Francisco: Jossey-Bass, John Wiley & Sons.

Coeling, H., & Cukr, P. (1997). What's happening: Don't underestimate your collaboration skills. *Journal of the American Academy of Nurse Practitioners, 9*, 515–520.

Cohen L., Baer N., & Satterwhite P. (2002). Developing effective coalitions: an eight step guide. In *Community health education & promotion: A guide to program design and evaluation* (2nd ed.), M. E. Wurzbach, Ed. Gaithersburg, MD: Aspen Publishers, pp. 144–161.

Kramer, M., & Schmalenberg, C. (2003). Securing "good" nurse physician relationship. *Nursing Management, 34*, 34–38.

Lindeke, L., & Block, D. (1998). Maintaining professional integrity in the midst of interdisciplinary collaboration. *Nursing Outlook, 46*, 213–218.

Lasker, R. D., & Committee on Medicine and Public Health. (1997). *Medicine & public health. The power of collaboration*. New York: New York Academy of Medicine.

Mitchell, P. H., Crittenden, R. A. (2000). Interdisciplinary collaboration: Old ideas with new urgency. *Washington Public Health, Fall*, 1–3.

Primary care in urban disadvantaged communities. (2004). J. Kai, & C. Drinkwater (Eds.). Abingdon, UK: Radcliffe Medical Press.

Robinson, A. (2004). Grassroots grants: An activist's guide to grant seeking (2nd ed.). Indianapolis, IN: Jossey-Bass.

Smoking. (2008). In *Encyclopedia Britannica*. Retrieved June 11, 2008, from Encyclopedia Britannica Online http://www.britannica.com/eb/article-242785

The Tony Grampsas Youth Services (TGYS). (2007). TGYS *Collaboration Assessment Toolkit*, Retrieved June 10, 2008 from the Colorado Department of Public Health and Environment Web site, http://www.cdphe.state.co.us/

Vickers, M. (2007). *The collaboration challenge. Trend Watcher Articles*. Retrieved October 13, 2008 from the Canadian Management Centre Web site, http://www.cmctraining.org/trendwatchers_view.asp?article_id=63

SUGGESTED READING

Center for the Advancement of Collaborative Strategies in Health (CACSH). (2003, updated 2007). *Medicine & public health: The power of collaboration*. Retrieved October 13, 2008 from http://www.cacsh.org/mph.html

Kay G., & Wolff, T. (1997). *From the ground up: A workbook on coalition building and community development*. Amherst: AHE/Community Partners.

CHAPTER 7

Complementary, Alternative, and Integrative Health Care Perspectives

The Executive Committee, Academic Consortium for Complementary and Alternative Health Care: John Weeks; Elizabeth Goldblatt, PhD, MHA/HA; Reed Phillips, DC, PhD; Pamela Snider, ND; Jan Schwartz, CMT; David O'Bryon, JD; Marcia Prenguber, ND; Donna Feeley, MPH, RN, LMT

Courtesy of the Academic Consortium for Complementary and Alternative Health Care (ACCAHC), from the Clinician's and Educator's Desk Reference on the Complementary and Alternative Health Care Professions, Elizabeth Goldblatt, Pamela Snider, John Weeks, editors (www.accahc.org)

LEARNING OBJECTIVES

After completing this chapter, the reader will be able to:

1. Provide basic information on complementary and alternative health care and integrative medicine.
2. Review factors which led to greater mainstream interest in these professionals and disciplines.

3. Understand the critical distinction between integrating therapies and integrating practitioners and disciplines.
4. Describe collaboratively established action areas in healthcare education for fostering mutual respect and understanding across the disciplines.
5. Present collaboratively established values to shape positive academic relationships between the disciplines.
6. Clarify basic elements of a curriculum to teach members of one discipline about another discipline.

KEY TERMS

Complementary and alternative health care
Complementary and alternative medicine (CAM)
Integrative medicine
Chiropractic
Acupuncture
Oriental medicine
Naturopathic medicine
Massage therapy
Academic Consortium for Complementary and Alternative Health Care (ACCAHC)
Direct-entry midwifery
Naturopathic physician (ND)
Acupuncture and Oriental medicine (AOM)
Doctor of chiropractic (DC)
Interinstitutional action
Holistic medicine
Holistic nursing
Consortium of Academic Health Centers for Integrative Medicine

INTRODUCTION

This chapter explores collaborative activity between educators in conventional academic medicine and educators involved with a set of distinctly licensed disciplines that, despite significant differences in origin and history, are commonly categorized by the dominant school of medicine as complementary and alternative medicine (CAM). The five disciplines with federally-recognized accrediting agencies are acupuncture and Oriental medicine (AOM), chiropractic, naturopathic medicine, direct-entry (homebirth) midwifery, and massage therapy. Educators for these disciplines prefer to be denominated as complementary and alternative *healthcare* disciplines, which is what we use here.

For these disciplines, significant local and national dialogue with conventional medical educators, and among themselves, has been engaged in only in the last decade. We begin with a description of some of the historical context for the emerging collaborative activity. Included here are recommendations from the White House Commission on Complementary and Alternative Healthcare Policy (NIH, 2002), from the Institute of Medicine (IOM, 2005), and from a multistakeholder and multidisciplinary national policy dialogue of a committee which became the Integrated Healthcare Policy Consortium (IHPC, 2002).

We then focus on the actions and directions set by the collaborative, *National Education Dialogue to Advance Integrated Health Care: Creating Common Ground* (Weeks et al., 2005) and the Academic Consortium for Complementary and Alternative Health Care (ACCAHC), for which we serve as the executive committee. (Both NED and ACCAHC were originally formed in 2004 as projects of the Integrated Healthcare Policy Consortium [Weeks et al., 2005]; ACCAHC is presently a distinct entity.) We also note some cross-disciplinary educational initiatives of some members of the conventional Consortium of Academic Health Centers for Integrative Medicine (CAHCIM), with 41 medical school members as of July 2008 (CAHCIM, 2006). The chapter includes priorities for action collaboratively established by these mixed groups of academics.

Additionally, we include some clarifying values, recommendations, and challenges we encountered on this road to bettering health care through deepened understanding and respect among educators across these disciplines.

DYNAMICS SHAPING THE EMERGING INTEREST IN COLLABORATION

Much of the interdisciplinary collaboration relative to complementary and alternative health care among academics, researchers, hospitals, community clinics, and other parts of our delivery system centers on relationships with members of five complementary and alternative healthcare professions. The five disciplines, as previously noted, are acupuncture and Oriental medicine (AOM), chiropractic, naturopathic medicine, direct-entry (homebirth) midwifery, and massage therapy.

These five disciplines have passed certain benchmarks of professional development. Success of each profession in achieving these benchmarks is typically a prerequisite for integration into the broader healthcare enterprise in the United States. Key steps are the creation of councils of colleges or schools, through which educational standards and an accrediting agency are established. This is followed by an effort to secure recognition of this agency by the United States Department of Education. Each profession also creates a national certifying or testing agency that is typically utilized by state regulators as the profession begins the long process of promoting licensing in each state. As is true for most medical fields, members of disciplines meeting these benchmarks are typically able to meet core credentialing standards for participation in conventional payment and delivery.

Table 7-1 provides data on the five complementary and alternative healthcare disciplines that have made significant advances in this benchmarking process. Focus is on the recognition of a federally-recognized accrediting agency. This benchmark typically signifies formal arrival not only academically for the discipline. The federal recognition of an accrediting body also offers reassurance to legislators considering licensing statutes.

Engagement between the complementary and alternative healthcare disciplines and conventional medical professionals has grown over the last two decades, yet is still in its infancy. A history of exclusion and antagonism that separated biomedicine from disciplines promoting holistic, integrative, and natural healthcare practices, while waning, still influences the dialogue. Residual misunderstandings, mistrust, and perhaps mostly ignorance from that era of polarization still can shadow efforts to create greater collaboration.

Table 7-2 offers a view of the way that the history of polarization can still affect interdisciplinary relationships. The bottom line in Table 7-2, as in past interdisciplinary experience, is that during the earlier nonintegrated era, patients whom each type of profession typically saw from other disciplines were their failures. Images of the other disciplines were therefore formed accordingly.

Table 7-1. Basic Information on the Licensed Complementary Healthcare Disciplines

Profession	Accrediting Agency Recognized by U.S. Department of Education	Total Number of Accredited Schools (2008)	Number of States with Licensing or Regulation	Total Number of Practitioners (estimated)
Acupuncture and Oriental medicine	1988	54	43	25,000
Chiropractic	1963	17	50	70,000
Massage therapy	2002	75*	39	250,000
Midwifery (direct-entry/ homebirth)	2001	10	24	1300
Naturopathic medicine	1987	5	15	3500

(*) The number reflects those accredited through the nationally-recognized specialized accrediting agency for massage education. Others may be accredited through other agencies.

Source: Clinicians and Educators Desk Reference on the Licensed Complementary and Alternative Healthcare Professions (ACCAHC, 2008). © Academic Consortium for Complementary and Alternative Health Care. Reprinted with permission.

The rift is clearly on the mend. Many factors, including general sociocultural shifts toward an interest in holism, environmentalism, internationalism, and multicultural awareness created the basis of current collaborative potential. The way the opening occurred continues to shape the nature of current collaborative activity. The following developments merit special recognition.

Opening Through Force: An Antitrust Lawsuit

In 1990, the chiropractic profession concluded a 15-year antitrust battle against the American Medical Association (AMA), Wilk vs. the AMA. (Wilk) The chiropractors' grassroots campaign led to a determination that the AMA had engaged in illegal restraint of trade through such practices

Table 7-2. Bilateral Prejudice as an Operational Issue in Limiting the Integration of Complementary and Conventional Health Care

Phenomenon	Conventional Perspective	Complementary Perspective
Successful complementary treatment	placebo for self-limiting condition	proof of value of complementary care
Successful conventional treatment	proof of value of conventional care	suppresses problems or fails to address causes
Science in conventional medicine	our foundation	80–90% of procedures have no support for clinical efficacy
Science in complementary medicine	virtually nonexistent	strong in some areas; growing body of evidence
Conventional primary care formulary	good tools	70% of problems go away on their own
Complementary primary care formulary	70% of problems go away on their own	good tools
Complementary diagnostics	of great concern; likely to misdiagnose	consider more than lab values
Conventional therapeutics	best in the world	often inappropriately invasive; likely to miss causes
Surgeon quick to operate	overutilizer	rip off artist
Chiropractor always requesting 20 visits	rip off artist	overutilizer
Antibiotics for viral conditions	basically harmless treatment demanded by patients	harmful to the individual and the population
Complementary therapies in end-stage terminal conditions	waste of money; creates false hope	alleviate side-effects of conventional treatment; patients with transition
Oncologist creating new chemotherapeutic "cocktails"	brilliant clinician	experimenting with poison
Naturopath who mixes Asian and homeopathic treatments	totally wacko	brilliant clinician

(continues)

Table 7-2. Bilateral Prejudice as an Operational Issue in Limiting the Integration of Complementary and Conventional Health Care (continued)

Phenomenon	Conventional Perspective	Complementary Perspective
Self-healing	self-limiting condition, spontaneous remission	healing power of nature
Clients of the "other" who come to my office	their failures	their failures

Note: The table was created by John Weeks in 1996 and is reflective of early perceptions which framed the integration dialogue. The choice of language does not reflect ACCAHC's current values and approaches. Weeks noted in the original that the language did not reflect the judgments of all providers from one school or the other. They were meant as generalizations.

Source: Operational Issues in Incorporating Complementary and Alternative Therapies and Providers in Benefit Plans and Managed Care Organizations. *Prepared for the Workshop: Complementary and Alternative Medicine: Issues Impacting Coverage Decisions.* Sponsored by U.S. National Institutes of Health Office of Alternative Medicine, U.S. Agency for Health Care Policy and Research, and the Arizona Prevention Center at the University of Arizona Health Sciences Center; October 9, 1996. John Weeks; contracted paper, p. 45.

as excluding chiropractors from hospitals and forbidding AMA members from sharing patients with chiropractors. Ending the era in which the AMA branded not just chiropractors but all nonconventional practitioners as "quacks" or "frauds" created a potential for dialogue between conventional medicine and all of the "alternative" and "holistic" fields.

Notably, the remains of this former polarization are still warm as collaborative initiatives are promoted today. A generation of physicians educated in the earlier era is often in leadership in academic centers and hospitals. At the same time, many professionals in the complementary and alternative healthcare professions who entered their profession in the era of polarization are in leadership in their professional organizations and institutions. While some conventional and complementary professionals from that earlier time are readily embracing the integration process, a frequently heard joke line in the movement for more collaboration is that paradigms change when the old finally die. Younger physicians are typically more influenced by recent cultural trends and more likely to have personally used complementary approaches in their own care.

Public Interest and Demand

Certainly the most powerful force behind our current work to learn how to better collaborate was evidence from a survey that found that over a third of consumers in 1991 used some form of "unconventional medicine" (Eisenberg et al., 1993). Originally reported in the *New England Journal of Medicine* in January 1993 and then updated for the *Journal of the American Medical Association* in 1998 (Eisenberg et al., 1998), the findings stimulated a fundamental change in perception among public officials, politicians, and members of the media. It turned out that "them"—the alternative medicine users—was "us."

Exploration about how to take advantage of this consumer interest began among hospitals, academics, insurers, and employers. Subsequent national surveys suggest that between 35–65% of consumers currently use some form of CAM. Other surveys have found that individuals with chronic conditions are more likely to explore nonconventional options. The level of consumer use and estimates of cash payments for these services perked the interest of conventional stakeholders.

Introduction of Significant Research and Education Grants

In 1991, via a $2 million Congressional earmark sponsored by U.S. Senator Tom Harkin, the National Institutes of Health (NIH) was urged to begin exploring "unconventional medicine." This initiative became the Office of Alternative Medicine and, in 1998, the National Center for Complementary and Alternative Medicine (NCCAM). The nation's academic health centers, which had heretofore shown little interest in these fields, suddenly saw that money was a significant new factor in what was a consumer-led movement. This development also supported the interests of conventional academics who saw value in opening to more nonconventional practices.

NCCAM's annual budget is roughly $120 million for 2008, most of which is distributed as grants to conventional medical centers. Over a dozen significant grants have gone to conventional academic health centers for education-related projects, most to members of the Consortium of Academic Health Centers for Integrative Medicine. Some of these conventional medical schools have had distinctly-licensed complementary healthcare educators–researchers as advisers; some had AOM or chiropractic or massage or naturopathic institutions as partners. In many of these grants, NCCAM required applicants to have partnerships with complementary and alternative healthcare institutions. It is important to add that NCCAM subsequently awarded a series of grants to complementary healthcare academic institutions with a requirement that they have conventional partners. Most of the best practices in interinstitutional, collaborative action were funded through these NCCAM grants.

In short, a major influence for exploring collaboration was this infusion of federal money, through an NIH Center which was foisted on the NIH by Congressional action. Though some conventional academic leaders were empowered by this federal action to advance their personal interests or interests of their patients in complementary therapies, institutional motivation for collaboration was often financial, rather than a more substantive interest in integrating education and or care.

Expansion of Integrative Medicine in Conventional Academic Health Centers

Closely associated with the advent of research funding is the expansion of interest in what is now called "integrative medicine" inside conventional academic health centers. In 1991, just one conventional medical school was known to have any education relative to complementary and alternative medicine. By 1998, that number reached 75.

In 2001, a Consortium of Academic Health Centers for Integrative Medicine (CAHCIM, 2006) was formed by nine academic health centers. To join, a center needed to have the support at the Dean's level or above, and integrative medicine activity in at least two of the three core arenas of healthcare academics (education, research, and clinical services). By 2008, the number of members throughout North America had grown to 41 academic health centers. An organization of philanthropists, the Bravewell Collaborative provided significant backing for the emerging consortium. The development of CAHCIM created a new focal point for collaborative academic activity and shifted the landscape in the alternative medicine integration arena.

These factors each opened doors for change agents inside and outside of mainstream medicine who believe that health care could be improved through fostering collaboration between conventional professionals and members of disciplines that historically had been externalized. Most of these professionals were integrative-oriented medical doctors, nurses, or administrators, some of them cross-trained in a complementary and alternative healthcare discipline. Evidence of consumer use allowed these individuals to claim the high ground of being patient-centered as they promoted dialogue, integration, and collaboration.

Yet the ongoing work of these collaboratively-minded professionals, and their partners in the complementary and alternative healthcare disciplines, remains shaped by the limitations of these institutional motivators and the bureaucratic challenges of making change. Optimally, integrative action would be engaged by a desire to understand why patients have been drawn to these services, and how care outcomes could be bettered, or medical costs reduced, by understanding and integrating these heretofore externalized practitioners. Ongoing institutional commitment to supporting the significant educational, economic, and cross-cultural challenges of collaboratively exploring the optimal integration of these new practitioner types has often been minimal.

PROMPTINGS FROM A WHITE HOUSE COMMISSION, THE IOM, AND A POLICY INITIATIVE

More recently, three significant national initiatives provided intellectual and policy-related support for those who chose to begin promoting more exploration of interdisciplinary activity between conventional and complementary and alternative healthcare professions. The report of the White House Commission on Complementary and Alternative Policy (NIH, 2002) urged that:

> . . . agencies should convene conferences of the leaders of CAM, conventional health, public health, evolving health professions, and the public; of educational institutions; and of appropriate organizations to facilitate the establishment of CAM education and training guidelines. Subsequently, the guidelines should be made available to the states and professions for their consideration. (NIH, 2002, p. 99)

The Commission endorsed 10 guiding principles. One recognizes that "partnerships are essential to integrated health care." (NIH, p. xxiii) Cross-disciplinary understanding and respect is underscored: "Good health care requires teamwork among patients, healthcare practitioners (conventional and CAM) and researchers committed to creating optimal healing environments and to respecting the diversity of all healthcare traditions." (NIH, 2002, xxiii)

The *National Policy Dialogue to Advance Integrated Care: Finding Common Ground*, which also published its findings in 2002, made similar recommendations. This multidisciplinary and multistakeholder gathering of 60 leaders in integrated care reached consensus on this core recommendation in the area of education: "Establish a national consortium of conventional and CAM educators and practitioners." Such a consortium would:

> . . . identify a core education for all conventional and CAM educational institutions, created by educators from the respective institutions themselves to ensure that the healthcare professionals of the future understand what all systems of health care can offer. This will result in healthcare providers, both conventional and CAM, learning at an early point in their training what other systems and modalities offer. The consortium will develop educational standards to ensure that factual and accurate information is taught across all disciplines and that the type of information is in accordance with the teachings and principles of the respective disciplines. (Quinn & Traubs, 2002, p.12)

The policy-oriented gathering also foresaw the need for a special accrediting entity for continuing education, and ongoing governmental support for collaborative education:

> An interdisciplinary body will be created to accredit continuing education programs in CAM/IHC for all medical disciplines so that medical, nursing, pharmacy students, and other healthcare professional students and practitioners, whether conventional or CAM, continue to learn about and respect the value of CAM and integrative healthcare approaches. Federal support is necessary to fund training opportunities in integrative healthcare settings so that medical students and healthcare practitioners, whether conventional or CAM, can learn about integrative approaches in order to provide better and more cost-effective patient care. (Quinn & Traub, 2002, pp. 11–12)

Finally, the IOM published a report entitled *Complementary and Alternative Medicine in the United States* in 2005, which acknowledged both the growth of the field and the central importance of collaborative and interdisciplinary action:

> The level of integration of conventional and CAM therapies is growing. That growth generates the need for tools or frameworks to make decisions about which therapies should be provided or recommended, about which

> CAM providers to whom conventional medical providers might refer patients, and the organizational structure to be used for the delivery of integrated care. The committee believes that the overarching rubric that should be used to guide the development of these tools should be the goal of providing comprehensive care that is safe and effective, that is collaborative and interdisciplinary, and that respects and joins effective interventions from all sources. (IOM, 2002, p. 216)

The report speaks directly to the problems that may arise if "integrative medicine" confines itself to the best uses of distinct approaches and therapies instead of honoring a "medical pluralism" that respects significant differences in "epistemological framework(s)" of practitioners from different disciplines.

> Yet, care must be taken not to assume compatibility where none exists. Medical pluralism should be distinguished from the cooptation of CAM therapies by conventional medical practices (Kaptchuk & Eisenberg, 2001). Although some conventional medical practices may seek and achieve a genuine integration with various CAM therapies, the hazard of integration is that certain CAM therapies may be delivered within the context of a conventional medical practice in ways that dissociate CAM modalities from the epistemological framework that guides the tailoring of the CAM practice. If this occurs, the healing process is likely to be less effective or even ineffective, undermining both the CAM therapy and the conventional biomedical practice. This is especially the case when the impact or change intended by the CAM therapy relies on a notion of efficacy that is not readily measurable by current scientific means. (IOM, 2002, p. 175)

It is noteworthy that, while this comment urges respect for distinctions between the disciplines, the report itself focused more significantly on integration of therapies than on integration of disciplines. A search by medical journalist Elaine Zablocki found that, in the IOM's report, "CAM therapies" appears 299 times, "CAM practitioners" 66 times, "CAM professions" is used 8 times, and "CAM disciplines" is used twice (Zablocki, 2002). The internal dialogue that was framed was one of grafting truncated therapies rather than the integration of disciplines, with all of their distinct differences and cultures.

While the decisions of many consumers of medicine have already provided ample reason for members of our diverse disciplines to learn to interact more closely, these three national initiatives added a necessary gloss of policy and medical leadership.

INITIAL CONVENTIONAL EXPLORATIONS IN COLLABORATIVE EDUCATION

Between 2000 and 2005, 15 conventional medical schools received multi-year grants from the NIH NCCAM, as previously noted, as part of the Complementary and Alternative Education Project. The October 2007 issue of *Academic Medicine* (Volume 82, Number 10) devoted 50 pages to 9 reports based on these experiences. Of most relevance is an article by Nedrow and colleagues (2007) about the four academic health centers that formed collaborative partnerships with nearby academic institutions that train CAM practitioners.

Developers of these collaborative programs note that respect for the potential value of complementary and alternative healthcare practitioners is linked to giving conventional practitioners direct experience of these distinctly licensed caregivers in educational, clinical, and research settings. Medical students at Georgetown University, for instance, report surprise in learning, during shared gross anatomy lab, the high level of understanding that massage therapists are required to achieve (Weeks, 2006). Confidence of medical students in working with complementary healthcare practitioners increased significantly with experience of the therapies among a group of medical students at the University of Minnesota (Weeks, 2006).

Nedrow's integrative medicine program at the Oregon Health and Science University forged ties with Western States Chiropractic College, National College of Natural Medicine (where the dominant program is in naturopathic medicine), and Oregon College of Oriental Medicine to form the Oregon Collaborative for Complementary and Integrative Medicine. Nedrow's conscious effort to put all of the participants in a nonhierarchical relationship, dubbed *lateral integration*, was well-received by the complementary healthcare educators. Nedrow has reported that barriers between professionals of different disciplines can be diminished when it is educators who are seeking to collaborate. The shared mission of educators to optimize the education of their students becomes the basis for open-minded collaboration.

Nedrow and her coauthors anticipate that such collaborations will increase. A key emerging issue they identified is credentialing of complementary healthcare practitioners to teach within conventional health professional institutions. The authors recognize that collaboration involves development of respect even in a context of significant differences. One proposed solution is to teach complementary health care "as an aspect of cultural sensitivity."

One sign of emerging openness to collaboration with members of other disciplines is that by 2007, the conventional Consortium for which Nedrow and her coauthors have been leaders, included participants who are faculty members of the medical schools who are also licensed members of the chiropractic, AOM, and naturopathic medical professions. These are presently serving on CAHCIM working groups and participating in their annual conferences.

ENGAGING A NATIONAL MULTIDISCIPLINARY COLLABORATION

In 2004 amidst this rapidly developing environment, the National Education Dialogue to Advance Integrated Health Care: *Creating Common Ground* (NED) was engaged. Most of us were involved in this process through the parallel creation of the multidisciplinary Academic Consortium for Complementary and Alternative Health Care (ACCAHC; 2008). ACCAHC was initially a means of clarifying issues between the mainstream and complementary healthcare disciplines. By design, many of the leaders of the conventional consortium, CAHCIM, were also involved in the 25-member planning team. NED ultimately included educators from 13 disciplines at a 4 day meeting of 75 educators in mid-2005 (see Box 7-1).

The 15 months of NED planning revolved around identification and engagement of a series of projects designed to inform the content of the on-site meeting. A first project was a survey of all of CAHCIM's integrative medicine programs (then 28) and all of the accredited schools and programs from the ACCAHC disciplines (then 130) to gain baseline data on the "Status of Inter-Institutional Relationships between CAM Disciplines and Conventional Integrative Medicine Programs" (Quinn & Traub, 2002, p.28). Sample findings included:

- Few of the then 28 CAHCIM member programs had formal classroom or clinical relationships with any complementary and alternative healthcare schools or colleges. Most involvement was found with AOM schools (32% classroom and 16% clinical) and massage schools (20% classroom and 20% clinical).

Box 7-1. Disciplines of Educator Participants in the National Education Dialogue

Acupuncture and Oriental medicine*	Midwifery (direct-entry)*
Chiropractic*	Naturopathic medicine*
Holistic medicine	Nutrition and dietetics
Holistic nursing	Occupational medicine
Homeopathic medicine	Osteopathic medicine
Integrative medicine	Public health
Massage therapy*	Yoga therapy*

* ACCAHC core disciplines. Yoga therapy, while not a licensed practice, is involved as an emerging, Traditional World Medicine discipline.

- Belief that developing "stronger, multidimensional, interdisciplinary relationships" is key to creating a "fully integrated healthcare system" was strong. Eighty-five percent of CAHCIM respondents and 86% of the ACCAHC respondents agreed.
- Sharing documents and strategies on best practices was viewed as the most beneficial strategy to support more interinstitutional relationships (73% of CAHCIM and 77% of ACCAHC).

In addition, a set of questions on the survey directed only at ACCAHC programs found that a majority of respondents have diverse clinical care relationships with conventional delivery organizations. Among these are community clinics (48%), hospitals (28%), senior homes (43%), and homeless clinics (33%). Such participation was highest in the naturopathic medical field, followed by chiropractic and AOM. The data were used to suggest that exploration of educational programs around integrated clinical services might take place in these existing "third-party" environments, many of which are already linked to conventional residencies and other placements.

Clarifying the Core Competencies of Integrative Medicine

A second multidisciplinary survey was stimulated by response of ACCAHC participants to the publication of a paper on competencies in integrative medicine, endorsed by CAHCIM, in *Academic Medicine* (Kligler et al., 2004). The paper was developed internally by CAHCIM, without input from leaders of the ACCAHC disciplines. A modified Delphi survey administered to a subset of 18 complementary healthcare educators from all ACCAHC core disciplines eventually elicited 5 key areas of concern with the competencies endorsed by CAHCIM (Benjamin et al., 2007). Most of the issues related to the core issue of integration were not merely concerned with "therapies" but an active engagement between diverse disciplines. The survey found that

> - The CAHCIM paper leaves the impression that conventional medical physicians may simply incorporate into their practices what they perceive to be good CAM therapies rather than referring to or co-managing and collaborating with CAM providers . . .
> - The CAHCIM paper does not include the option of integrated care with MDs and CAM practitioners as partners, and seems to propose that CAM be an add-on to conventional medical care.
> - Occasionally in the paper language appears to reflect a continuation of the 'us and them' mindset rather than seeing that CAM providers, faculty, and systems could and should be part of IM.
> - The paper gives the impression that conventional medical institutions want to include CAM, but not necessarily CAM practitioners, in their vision of IM.
> - CAM is defined in relationship to biomedicine as complementary or alternative, but is considered integrative if delivered by conventional physicians.
>
> (Benjamin et al., 2007, p. 1023)

The issue of the distinction between integration of "therapies" versus the more challenging and the significantly more beneficial work of collaboration between disciplines led to a process in which CAHCIM changed its definition of "integrative medicine" to better reflect the importance of working with other disciplines (see Box 7-2).

Efforts to Create Shared Values to Guide Interdisciplinary Action

A third project, led by holistic nurse educator Carla Mariano, RN, EdD, BC-HN, sought to clarify a shared set of values across the disciplines involved with the NED process. The vision behind this project was of a document that might be coproduced by a multidisciplinary NED team and endorsed by the NED planning committee, and then amended and endorsed by the onsite gathering of 75 educators. Once agreement was reached, this document would then be taken to the individual disciplines for endorsement as a shared basis for interdisciplinary action. The operating belief of the 10 educators from 8 disciplines who comprised the "Values,

Box 7-2. From Integration of Therapies to Collaboration Among Disciplines

The planning team for the National Education Dialogue (NED) to Advance Integrated Health Care: *Creating Common Ground* was an alphabet soup of titles never before gathered for a shared educational purpose. These included MD, ND (naturopathic physician), LAc (AOM practitioner), MPH, DC (doctor of chiropractic), PhD, LM (licensed midwife), RN, LMT (licensed massage therapist), and RYT (registered yoga teacher).

The hope and expectation among educators and practitioners was that such educational collaboration would then translate into more understanding and cooperation among practitioners. The organizing mantra was *those who are educated together practice together*. What could educators do to help get their disciplines out of separate silos and break down the historic barriers between "conventional" and "alternative" professions? An early step was to clarify what shared vision, if any, unified the leaders. The group agreed on this statement:

> We envision a health care system that is multidisciplinary and enhances competence, mutual respect and collaboration across all complementary and alternative medicine and conventional health care disciplines. This system will deliver effective care that is patient centered, focused on health creation and healing, and readily accessible to all populations. (Weeks et al., 2005, p. 1)

A funny thing happened on the way to working on this vision. On the December 2004 NED planning team call, one of these planners announced that at the recent general meeting of CAHCIM, the conventionally-based academics agreed on a definition of "integrative medicine."

> Integrative medicine is the practice of medicine that reaffirms the importance of the relationship between practitioner and patient, focuses on the whole person, is informed by evidence, and makes use of all appropriate therapeutic approaches to achieve optimal health and healing. (Weeks et al, 2005: p.16)

The success of representatives from the then 25 medical schools to come to agreement on a definition of their field had taken months of committee work. The eight members of the planning team who also were members of CAHCIM were congratulated.

But this definition was not well received by many on the call. The first issue was participatory: If "integrative medicine" was to be inclusive, then why were not leaders of other disciplines asked to collaborate on establishing the definition? The second issue was substantive and went to the heart of collaboration. Where, in that definition, was the evidence that a practitioner of "integrative medicine" must, in the words of the NED vision, be "multidisciplinary and enhance(s) competence, mutual respect, and collaboration across all complementary and alternative medicine and conventional healthcare disciplines?"

(continues)

Box 7-2. From Integration of Therapies to Collaboration Among Disciplines (continued)

One responsibility the ACCAHC had in the NED process was to articulate and advance shared issues with the cultural-medical shift toward more integrated health care. That the definition of integrative medicine included no reference to the importance of knowing how to collaborate with other types of healthcare professionals and disciplines was one issue. The word "approach," for instance, disrespected the unique contributions of practitioners licensed to practice the 4000-year-old discipline of acupuncture and Oriental medicine.

ACCAHC members asked their CAHCIM colleagues to change their definition of integrative medicine. The request was well received. A conventional colleague noted that the IOM of the National Academies, in a report on Complementary and Alternative Medicine in the United States, had underscored the importance of care that is "collaborative and interdisciplinary and that respects and joins effective interventions from all sources." The CAHCIM definition was formally amended to read:

> Integrative Medicine is the practice of medicine that reaffirms the importance of the relationship between practitioner and patient, focuses on the whole person, is informed by evidence, and makes use of all appropriate therapeutic approaches, healthcare professionals and disciplines to achieve optimal health and healing. (Weeks et al, 2005; p.16)

In short, "integrative medicine" requires more than integration of the "appropriate therapeutic approaches." Practitioners must also know how to make the best use of "healthcare professionals and disciplines" to achieve optimal health and healing. Notably, the amended definition also elevated the status of all "non-CAM" disciplines including nurses, physical therapists, psychologists, nutritionists, and others. A definitional platform was laid for an emerging vision of a healthcare system which asserts that reform will require all disciplines to recognize that they must, of necessity, work as part of respectful, collaborative teams.

Knowledge, Skills and Attitudes Task Force" was that the process of shifting the disciplines out of their historic isolation would benefit from a collaboratively developed guiding document.

Through a series of phone meetings and small group work, a draft statement of "Core Values" was developed. These were coupled with listed "Examples of Knowledge" and "Examples of Skills" that were viewed as associated with each of the values. The Task Force as a group endorsed the statements as a working document. The "Core Values" served as the basis of an intensely interactive World Café format for the 75 educators at the on-site NED meeting (see Box 7-3). Participants at the gathering also proved to

Box 7-3. Core Values to Word Shaping Collaboration in Integrated Care

WHOLENESS AND HEALING

We acknowledge and value the interconnectedness of all people and all things. We believe that healing is an innate, although sometimes mysterious, capacity of every individual, which provides a meaningful opportunity for growth and balance, even when curing may not be possible.

CLIENTS/PATIENTS/FAMILIES

We value our clients/patients/families as the center of our practices. We act in service to validate individuals' full experience of their wellness and illness, provide education about the possibilities for change, diminish dependence, bolster resilience, support the mobilization of their full resources, and reinforce self-reliance as important to optimal healing.

PRACTICE AS COMBINED ART AND SCIENCE

We value competent, compassionate, relationship-centered practice that honors intuitive knowledge, stimulates creativity in the face of divergent circumstances, and appropriately utilizes a network of diverse practitioners as integral to the practice of the healing arts. This approach is informed by in-depth education, critical thinking, reliable evidence from well-designed quantitative and qualitative research, and by respect for diverse theories and world views.

SELF-CARE OF THE PRACTITIONER

We value a practitioner's commitment to self-reflection, self-care, and to his or her personal growth and healing as being essential to one's humble ability to provide the most effective and enduring health care to others.

INTERDISCIPLINARY COLLABORATION AND INTEGRATION

We embrace the breadth and depth of diverse healthcare systems and value collaboration of all providers within and across disciplines and with clients/patients and their families. We believe that fostering integrative and collaborative practice is essential to the creation of health, the advancement of health care, and the wellbeing of society.

OUR HEALTH SYSTEM

We value the recognition that all practitioners have responsibility to participate in activities that contribute to the improvement of the community, the

(continues)

Box 7-3. Core Values to Word Shaping Collaboration in Integrated Care (continued)

environment and the betterment of public health. We support access for all populations to competent client/patient-centered care, which is focused on health creation and healing. We believe that advancement and promotion of health and the prevention of disease are fostered by aligning resource investment with these values.

ATTITUDES AND BEHAVIORS THAT PROMOTE HEALTH, WELLNESS, AND CHANGE

We value attitudes and behaviors that demonstrate respect for self and others and that are informed by an abiding humility, in light of both the individual care and system challenges that we face. We value authentic, open and courageous communication. We believe that such traits are important for all participants in health care, whether practitioner, client/patient/family, educator, administrator, or policy-maker.

Note: A multidisciplinary team of educators from eight disciplines collaborated in a series of conference calls to propose the preceding as a set of values that would guide disciplines in integrated health care. While never formally endorsed by the disciplines involved in the National Education Dialogue meeting, these remain a good framework for collaboration.

Source: Developed through an ACCAHC and National Education Dialogue team chaired by Carla Mariano, RN, EdD, BC-HN and including Michael Goldstein, PhD; Ben Kligler, MD, MPH; Karen Lawson, MD; David O'Bryon, JD; Mark Seem, LAc; Dawn Schmidt, LMP; Pamela Snider, ND; Don Warren, ND, DHANP; and John Weeks (2005).

be a long way from consensus. The group also had contradictory feelings about the ultimate contribution such a document might have, yet an onsite survey strongly supported continuing the work "to create a concise statement of core values which have resonance across the disciplines and can guide efforts to create quality integrated healthcare education"(Weeks et al, 2005, p. 3).

A reconstituted Task Force continued work via a series of phone meetings after the onsite meeting. They found two resources of particular value in guiding their activity together. One is the section on Practitioner to Practitioner Relationships in the Pew-Fetzer's seminal document on relationship-centered care (Tresolini, 1994; see Table 7-3). Particularly noteworthy are issues related to knowledge of self, ability to understand the

Table 7-3. Practitioner to Practitioner Relationships in Relationship-Centered Care

Area	Knowledge	Skills	Values
Self-awareness	• Knowledge of self	• Reflect on self and needs • Learn continuously	• Importance of self-awareness
Traditions of knowledge in health professions	• Healing approaches of various professions and across cultures • Historical power inequities across professions	• Derive meaning from others' work • Learn from experience in a healing community	• Affirmation and value of diversity
Building teams and communities	• Perspectives on team building from the social sciences	• Communicate effectively • Listen openly • Learn cooperatively	• Affirmation of mission • Affirmation of diversity
Working dynamics of teams and communities	• Perspectives on team dynamics from the social sciences	• Share responsibility responsibly • Collaborate with others • Work cooperatively • Resolve conflicts	• Openness to others' ideas • Humility • Mutual trust, empathy, support • Capacity for grace

Source: Tresolini C.P. and the Pew-Fetzer Task Force. *Health Professions Education and Relationship-Centered Care*. San Francisco, CA: Pew Health Professions Commission. 1994; p. 36.

"historical power inequities across the professions," "affirmation of the value of diversity," and the importance of team dynamics.

The second guiding document for the team's work to deepen understanding between the disciplines was the "Four Quadrants" from Ken Wilber's *Integral Theory of Consciousness* (Wilbur, 1997). The group quickly noticed that much of the integration activity has been shaped by the right quadrants. These are related to exterior inputs such as randomized controlled trials, publications, and capacity to participate. The Values Working Group engaged an internal process that explored the way that subjective issues such as self-knowledge, personal involvement in health, and appreciation of the diversity of professional experience and culture, such as those noted in the Pew-Fetzer document, influence collaborative behavior.

Remedial Need: Model Education Tools on the Disciplines

We recognized that much of the early work we need is remedial. Practitioners of one healthcare system cannot effectively collaborate with practitioners of other systems unless they possess knowledge and understanding about the various healthcare disciplines that exist. The decades of separation between conventional and complementary healthcare disciplines, between the mind and body, and between the physical location of our educational institutions and clinics, underscored the importance of such education. A well-formulated survey course, or set of courses, would provide an important basis for opening hearts and minds to the "other," to encourage collaboration to better serve patients.

The specific ways in which collaboration can be enhanced through such training about other disciplines are numerous. Dialogue opens. Practitioners become better able to discuss healthcare options outside of the practitioner's own field, with both patients and other practitioners. They can better understand treatments patients may already be receiving from other healthcare practitioners. Cross-referral will be enhanced as practitioners develop openness to other medical cultures and paradigms. Potential to work successfully in multidisciplinary healthcare settings and on collaborative research projects will be enhanced.

Box 7-4 is based on work led by Elizabeth Goldblatt, PhD, MHA/PA, and Daniel Seitz, JD, involving a team of eight professionals from four disciplines that was presented at the NED onsite gathering.

To create a significant understanding, representatives of each discipline preferred to see requirements of at least 2 to 3 credits or 30 to 45 course hours on each discipline. However, already bulging educational requirements in conventional healthcare professions and in complementary healthcare education effectively vetoed an approach that recommended inclusion as core curriculum. A compromise recommendation, though still a challenge to fit, is a survey course of 30 to 45 contact hours in which all of the licensed complementary healthcare disciplines are examined.

Box 7-4. Topics and Suggested Formats in Education on the Distinctly Licensed Complementary and Alternative Healthcare Professions

EDUCATIONAL TOPICS

- Basic philosophy about health and healing or core values of the discipline
- Basic theory of the discipline and any unique terminology
- History and current status of the field
- Status of research in the field, review of the literature, evidence-based material, cultural issues that may restrict or enhance research and research priorities identified by the profession
- Strengths and limitations in preventing and treating conditions, and promoting health
- Educational training requirements, competencies
- Institutional and programmatic accreditation practices
- Certification and examination agencies and processes
- Professional licensing and scope of practice
- Credentialing issues in hospitals and third-party payment
- Experience in comanagement and referral strategies
- Best practices in integration with other practitioners
- Bibliography of recommended additional resources

ACTIVITIES AND EDUCATIONAL FORMATS

- Lecture and case demonstrations on how the discipline approaches specific cases (best practices, strengths and weaknesses, working alone, working collaboratively)
- Joint case discussions in which specific cases are presented from the perspectives of a variety of disciplines
- Directly experiencing different forms of health care, such as receiving acupuncture and Oriental medicine treatments, chiropractic adjustments, nutrition and diet assessments, massage therapy, and the whole-person naturopathic intake
- Grand rounds-type observations in integrative clinics
- Develop a few "simple" techniques that can be incorporated into self-care
- Explore how to work collaboratively and case-manage with other healthcare providers

Based on materials developed by Elizabeth (Liza) Goldblatt, PhD, MPA/HA and Daniel Seitz, JD, MAT, with an ACCAHC and the National Education Dialogue team who also included Frank Zolli, DC, EdD; Adam Perlman, MD; Pamela Snider, ND; Don Warren, ND; and John Weeks.

Recognizing that even this is a push for many educational programs, after the NED meeting the ACCAHC developed two resources. One is a small book entitled *The Clinicians & Educators Desk Reference on the Complementary and Alternative Healthcare Professions.* The second, based on the book, is a two-hour short course that introduces professionals to the licensed disciplines. Both are available through the Internet (ACCAHC, 2008).

Priority Recommendations for Interdisciplinary Educational Collaboration

After 15 months of planning and collaborative project execution, 3 days onsite, and 2 surveys of participants, the National Education Dialogue to Advance Integrated Health Care identified 9 priority areas for action in which there was significant "common ground" (>80% agreement; Weeks et al., 2005, p. 3).

- Facilitate development of interinstitutional relationships and geographically-based groupings of conventional and CAM institutions and disciplines in diverse regions. Promote student and faculty exchanges, create new clinical opportunities, facilitate integrated postgraduate and residency programs, and provide opportunities for students to audit classes and share library privileges.
- Create resource modules on teaching about distinct CAM, conventional and emerging disciplines (approved by the disciplines), which can be used in a variety of formats from supporting materials in such areas as definitions and glossaries to full curricular modules.
- Share educational and faculty resources and information on interinstitutional relationships, including samples of existing agreements and existing educational resources through development of a Web site.
- Continue multidisciplinary work to create a concise statement of core values that have resonance across the disciplines and can guide efforts to create quality integrated healthcare education.
- Collaboratively develop and sponsor continuing education initiatives designed to draw participants from diverse disciplines.
- Create collaboratively developed educational resources to prepare students and practitioners to practice in integrated clinical settings.
- Develop an outline of skills and attitudes appropriate for those involved in collaborative integrated health care.

- Assist individuals with making institutional changes by offering support for leadership in change creation. Explore strategies for overcoming the challenges of prejudice, ignorance, and cultural diversity.
- Explore third-party clinical sites that serve the underserved (such as community health centers) as locations for developing clinical education in integrated healthcare practices.

Collaboration After the NED Meeting

Significant efforts were made to find philanthropic support that would allow the NED teams to remain intact and begin fulfilling on these priorities. Limited funds were raised to advance the values initiative and some interdisciplinary collaboration, yet the broader NED effort was suspended roughly a year later. While NED was still robust, the effort's epitaph was provided by the chair of the IOM committee that had produced the 2005 report on complementary and alternative healthcare in the United States: "What you are doing [with NED], this great collaborative work, is one of the most important things anyone can do to implement this report"(Weeks et al., 2005, p.1).

ACCAHC Collaborative Activity After the NED Meeting Meantime, the educators from the complementary and alternative healthcare disciplines decided to commit to establishing ACCAHC as an ongoing agency for fostering academic collaboration that can lead to enhanced, better integrated patient care. ACCAHC was incorporated as a 501c3 organization. Table 7-4, ACCAHC Organizational Members as of August 2008, shows that the potential for the organization has been embraced by most of the relevant organizations associated with the licensed complementary and alternative healthcare disciplines. Its operational funding is from member dues and from philanthropic grants.

As ACCAHC's organizational structure was developed, the participants wanted to be sure that there would be provisions for inclusion of those complementary and alternative professions, which were seeking to engage the self-regulatory and regulatory processes that allow it to play a more significant part in healthcare delivery. Concerns were voiced that without such a provision, ACCAHC would recapitulate the pattern of exclusion that had added to the challenge of each of their own maturation processes. ACCAHC chose to open its doors to allow organizations in two categories—Traditional

World Medicines (TWM) and Emerging Professions—to participate and learn from ACCAHC's core members. To date, this provision has allowed organizations representing two TWM organizations, representing Yoga therapists and registering Yoga teachers and schools, to join. Other discussions are underway.

ACCAHC's interdisciplinary work to better health care is divided between projects focusing on expanding collaboration internally, between the member disciplines, and serving as a platform for engaging projects with conventional colleagues. ACCAHC's operating structure consists of the board, an executive committee, an Education Working Group, Clinical Care Working Group, and Research Working Group, each of which consists of 12 to 16 representatives from ACCAHC member disciplines and from the public. This structure was deliberately established to parallel the structure of the conventional consortium, the Consortium of Academic Health Centers for Integrative Medicine (CAHCIM). Discussions on placing representatives on each others' working groups were under way as this chapter was written. In addition, to facilitate communication and collaboration, ACCAHC established special interest groups (SPIGs), which support relationship development among organizations from ACCAHC's distinct member types (councils of colleges and other schools, accrediting agencies, and certification and testing organizations). A Student Organization Leadership SPIG was formed to foster relationships between students across the ACCAHC disciplines. In planning at this writing are a multidisciplinary institution SPIG for those institutions offering more than one academic program, some of which have transitioned to become universities of natural health sciences, and a TWM SPIG.

Among projects underway are: development of educational materials on the disciplines; fostering interest in collaborative action to advance team health care among educators; supporting consumer interest in distinctly licensed practitioners in a National Summit on Integrative Medicine and the Health of the Public sponsored by the IOM; creating forums to foster greater exchange on multidisciplinary aspects of patient-centered care between the leaders of the member organizations; linking student leaders across the disciplines; exploring a leadership-oriented, multidisciplinary course to develop collaborative skills in a subset of students; supporting the development of a stronger research ethos in ACCAHC's educational institutions; and engaging sponsors of continuing medical education on

Table 7-4. ACCAHC Organizational Members as of October 2008

Member Type	Member Organizations
Councils of Colleges and Schools	Council of Colleges of Acupuncture and Oriental Medicine Association of Chiropractic Colleges American Massage Therapy Association-Council of Schools Association of Accredited Naturopathic Medical Colleges
Accrediting Agencies	Commission on Massage Therapy Accreditation Council on Chiropractic Education Council on Naturopathic Medical Education Midwifery Education Accreditation Council
Testing and Certification Organizations	North American Board of Naturopathic Examiners National Certification Board for Therapeutic Massage and Bodywork National Certification Commission for Acupuncture and Oriental Medicine (affiliate member only) National Board of Chiropractic Examiners (affiliate member only)
Traditional World Medicines and Emerging Professions*	International Association of Yoga Therapists Yoga Alliance

Members pay dues based on organizational revenue.

* The Traditional World Medicine category of organizational member was created to allow participation of professions that are engaging in the educational and professional self-regulatory and regulatory efforts that most of the other complementary and alternative disciplines (core members) had engaged in during the prior two decades.

Source: © Academic Consortium for Complementary and Alternative Health Care. Reprinted with permission.

integrative medicine to offer content which will foster better team care and collaboration among professionals.

CONCLUSION

The past decade has seen significant development of the values and definitional commitments as well as the operational infrastructure that is expected to support collaborative action for integrative medicine and the licensed complementary and alternative healthcare professions for decades to come.

Collaborative action is already growing rapidly, given the historic estrangement between many of these fields. An ongoing challenge is to show how patients can benefit when practitioners of different stripes are not merely viewed as purveyors of therapies but as exponents of entire disciplines with their own rich histories and distinct approaches to patient care. A practical requirement is creating strategies for enriching cross-disciplinary experience amidst curricular demands that are already overflowing. To urge respect for whole practices that are respectful of mind-body-spirit approaches by piling additional coursework on burdened health professional students is an uncomfortable paradox. Yet multiple forces in the broader culture energize this effort. These range from cultural shifts and consumer interests to top level reports on the importance of collaboration in the treatment of costly chronic diseases. Patient-centered care, patient–practitioner partnership, and team medicine are all elements of renewed efforts to create a medical system which is proactive and focuses on health creation.

A frequently quoted statement among academic researchers around integrative and complementary medicine themes is that one day we will no longer have "conventional medicine" and "alternative medicine," only good medicine. Such a rosy resolution of the philosophical debates on diverse approaches to health and medicine that go back not just decades but centuries may not be anticipated in the near future. However, that we learn to collaborate more respectfully despite our differences may be a part of "good medicine" that is a necessary antecedent to clarity on the rest.

DISCUSSION QUESTIONS

1. Describe how more experience with other disciplines in the course of health professional education is a necessary antecedent to optimal collaboration as a clinician.

2. What are examples of subjective or cultural issues that may influence the ability of members of one discipline from understanding or working with members of another discipline?
3. What is the significance of the amendment to the definition of "integrative medicine" developed by the Consortium of Academic Health Centers for Integrative Medicine?
4. How would collaboration be enhanced if leaders of all the disciplines endorsed a shared set of core values?
5. Why might community clinics rather than academic health centers be good locations for exploring educational strategies in the area of clinical collaboration?
6. What has motivated mainstream healthcare institutions to explore integration of complementary and alternative medicine? How might these motivations shape the collaborative opportunities?
7. What were the concerns expressed by the complementary healthcare educators about the competencies in integrative medicine being labeled and endorsed by conventional integrative medicine educators?
8. What knowledge or information would you want to have about a discipline in order to feel comfortable referring to a member of that discipline?

REFERENCES

Academic Consortium for Complementary and Alternative Health Care. (2008). *Welcome to ACCAHC.* Accessed October 14, 2008 from http://www.accahc.org/

Benjamin P. J., Phillips R., Warren D., Salveson C., Hammerschlag R., Snider P., & Haas M. (2007). Response to a proposal for an integrative medicine curriculum. *Journal of Alternative and Complementary Medicine, 13*, 1021–1033.

Consortium of Academic Health Centers for Integrative Medicine (CAHCIM). (2006). Homepage. Accessed October 14, 2008 from http://www.imconsortium.org/

Eisenberg, D. M., Kessler, R. C., Foster, C., Norlock F. E., Calkins, D. R., & Delbanco, T. L. (1993). Unconventional medicine in the United States—Prevalence, costs, and patterns of use. *New England Journal of Medicine, 328*, 246–252.

Eisenberg, D.M., Davis, R. B., Ettner, S. L., Appel, S., Wilkey, S., Van Rompey, M., & Kessler, R. C. (1998) Trends in Alternative Medicine Use in the United States, 1990–1997. *JAMA, 280*, 1569–1575.

Institute of Medicine (IOM) of the National Academies. (2005). *Committee on the Use of Complementary and Alternative Medicine by the American Public, Board on Health Promotion and Disease Prevention, Complementary and Alternative Medicine in the United States.* Washington, DC: National Academies Press.

Integrated Healthcare Policy Consortium (IHPC, 2002). Accessed February 23, 2009 at www.ihpc.info

Kaptchuk T. J., & Eisenberg, D. M. (2001). Varieties of healing. 1: Medical pluralism in the United States. *Annals of Internal Medicine, 135*, 189–195.

Kligler B., Maizes V., Schachter S., Park C., Gaudet T., Benn R., Lee R., & Remen R. N. (2004). Core competencies in integrative medicine for medical school curricula: A proposal. *Academic Medicine, 79*, 521–531.

National Institutes of Health (NIH). (2002). *White House Commission on Complementary and Alternative Medicine Policy.* NIH Publication 03-5411; ISBN 0-16-051476-2.

Nedrow, A. R., Heitkemper, M., Frenkel, M., Mann, D., Wayne P., & Hughes E. (2007). Collaborations between allopathic and complementary and alternative medicine health professionals: Four initiatives. *Academic Medicine, 82*, 962–966.

Quinn, S., & Traub M. (Eds.). (2002). *National Policy Dialogue to Advance Integrated Health Care; Finding Common Ground.* Steering Committee for the National Policy Dialogue, Integrated Health Care Consortium. Retrieved October 14, 2008 from http://ihpc.info/resources/NPDFR.pdf

Tresolini C. P., & The Pew-Fetzer Task Force. (1994). *Health Professions Education and Relationship-Centered Care.* San Francisco, CA: Pew Health Professions Commission, p. 36. © The Pew Health Commission and the Fetzer Institute. Retrieved October 14, 2008 from http://www.futurehealth.ucsf.edu/pdf_files/Relationship Centered.pdf

Weeks J., Snider P., Quinn S., O'Bryon, D., Haramati, A., et al. (2005) *National Education Dialogue to Advance Integrated Health Care: Creating Common Ground*: Progress Report, March 2004–September 2005. Retrieved October 14, 2008 from http://ihpc.info/resources/NEDPR.pdf

Weeks, J. (2006). The future of MD education: Empathy, roses and respect via Georgetown and U Minnesota pilots. *The Integrator Blog News & Reports, August 15, 2006.* Retrieved October 14, 2008 from http://theintegratorblog.com/site/index.php?option=com_content&task=view&id=128&Itemid=93

Wilbur, K. (1997). An integral theory of consciousness. *Journal of Consciousness Studies, 4*, 71–92. Retrieved October 14, 2008 from http://www.imprint.co.uk/Wilber.htm

Wilk v. American Medical Association. (1990). 895 F.2d 352 (7th Cir). Accessed October 14, 2008 from the Chiropractic Resource Organization, http://www.chiro.org/abstracts/amavschiro.pdf

Zablocki, E. (personal communication, June 2002).

Appendix: Case Studies

Two additional case studies are provided as examples of collaboration in health care and to initiate critical thinking, problem solving, decision making, and applied discussion in the classroom. The first is "Sandhills Hospitals," which illustrates the value, challenges, and successes of physician collaboration in a hospital setting. The second is "The Orange County Healthcare Needs Assessment."

> **INSTRUCTORS:**
>
> See the Jones and Bartlett Web site, http://www.jbpub.com/catalog/9780763755584/, for this text's online resources, including an Instructor's Manual with teaching notes and additional resources.

CASE STUDY 1

Sandhills Health Information Network: A Case Study in Hospital–Physician Collaboration

by Windsor Westbrook Sherrill, PhD, MBA, MHA
Associate Professor
Department of Public Health Sciences
Clemson University

LEARNING OBJECTIVES

After analyzing this case, the student should be able to:

1. Identify the critical role of collaboration between hospitals and physicians in implementing an integrated health service information network.
2. Identify success factors in collaboration between hospitals, physician groups, and information services vendors.
3. Articulate opportunities for and barriers to collaboration in the selection of, and the implementation and transition to an integrated health information network.

INTRODUCTION

Sandhills County, South Carolina is a rural region with a population of 67,000. The county has grown significantly in past years, largely due to two factors. A number of affluent retirees are settling in the Lakes region of the county, and migration into the area from northern states is steady. Although many retirees moving to the area are well insured, 10.8 percent of the population in the county lives below poverty level, and 21 percent of the population qualifies for public assistance. The population is 85 percent Caucasian, but Hispanic population growth is among the highest in the region. Per capita income for the area is just over $25,000. According to the BRFSS, 64 percent of the population in the county is overweight, and 24 percent of mothers do not receive adequate prenatal care. Health service providers in the area are faced with the dual challenges of caring for growing numbers of patients with chronic illness and absorbing decreasing third party reimbursements for care.

COLLABORATION IMPERATIVE: AN INTEGRATED HEALTH INFORMATION NETWORK

The vision of the Sandhills Health Information Network is "to improve the quality, safety and efficiency of health care delivery to people in our region through the secure exchange of health information among multiple health care providers." The challenge of the Network is to select, adopt, and implement a community-wide health information system serving the hospital, numerous individual providers, third-party payers and multiple other health care providers.

Plans for electronic health records and a connected health services community include three levels of service:

1. Infrastructure and secure access
2. Broadly adopted applications
3. Connectivity and interoperability

Integration offers the potential for health information connections among all members of the health services community: hospitals, ancillary departments, employers, physicians, homecare providers, patients, payors, and retail pharmacies. The network will provide improved outcomes for each of these constituents. Clinical outcomes will be enhanced with an environment providing continuity of care, and financial outcomes will be improved through the expected greater productivity, revenue enhancement, and cost reductions.

HISTORY OF THE ORGANIZATION

Sandhills Community Hospital has 160 beds and almost 10,000 inpatient discharges annually, and employs over 1,400 staff. The hospital is accredited by the Joint Commission and has been in operation for more than 65 years. One hundred and twenty physicians practice in the service area, a majority of whom have hospital privileges. Twenty-five specialties are represented on the medical staff. The hospital sponsors a hospice as well as a rural residency training program. Sandhills County Hospital is now undergoing a significant facility expansion with a new patient care tower and ancillary support facilities.

The challenge faced by the organization is to facilitate the development of an integrated health information network for the region.

The Sandhills Health Information Network was formed as a nonprofit collaboration among physicians and the hospital with a goal of building a health information exchange system to provide seamless communication among healthcare providers. This initiative is a partnership between area physicians and the hospital. The Network has the goal of adding measurable practice value and benefits for physicians and patients, the hospital and clinics, payors and the community served. The primary goals of the initiative are health process improvement through information automation, and quality improvement through collaboration and the adoption of best practice standards in information systems.

The first step in the transition to an integrated health information network has been completed. A request for proposals was submitted to information services vendors by the hospital and the steering committee of physician providers. One vendor was selected to begin the process of establishing a technology foundation for the network. The vendor worked in close collaboration with the hospital and provider organization.

During phase two, the steering group has been working to engage additional critical partners in the process. Specifically, payors, ancillary providers, retail pharmacies, and additional physicians in the region are to be brought on board as users of the information network.

The long-term plan is to extend the information network to patients, through secure messaging, Web-visits, and telehealth services. The vision of the network is to provide a cutting edge virtual healthcare organization across the entire community. With collaboration among the partners on this implementation of a successful network, the region can be a model for replication by other local area health networks. The network can provide leverage for potential state and federal funding as well as increased reimbursement from third party payers. It also will furnish the foundation for likely growth into a broader regional health information network.

Some difficulties have emerged during phase two of the process. Although many physician providers have purchased and adopted the technology, implementation has been challenging. The physician support package is seen as expensive for small groups or solo practice groups. Those who have purchased the products have experienced the pains of being "first adopters." The electronic medical record component of the product has to be tailored to each individual practice and specialty through a time-consuming process. Some practices have elected to take a "wait and see" approach to program implementation; others have purchased the Eletronic Medical Records (EMR) package without the decision support module. Those groups who are adopting the practice decision support system have commented that customer support for implementation needs to be individualized to each individual practice.

The hospital information support system is up and running, but the physicians groups are lagging in the anticipated implementation schedule.

The community-wide information network is far from complete, and two years have passed since the purchase of the original system by the hospital.

KEY PLAYERS

The different professional groups ("players") must work together on the shared problem of information networking toward a common goal of improving health service delivery in the region. Although a health information network can enhance patient care and eventually result in cost savings, the transition to the network is expensive and time-consuming.

To make the network successful, Sandhills Community Hospital needs the involvement of all providers in the region. Individual providers are burdened with increasing uncompensated patient loads as well as decreasing third party payments. Most providers are interested and supportive of the network but have limited practice and financial resources to commit to implementation.

INTERNAL SITUATION

The anticipated benefits for providers are increased operational efficiency, a streamlined health care delivery process through the sharing of personal health information, reduction of duplication of procedures and services, as well as reduction in costs, waste, fraud, and abuse. It is expected that this information network will facilitate increased HIPAA compliance, empower patients, and improve health quality, provider–patient communications, and community health outcomes.

Although providers are aware of the many potential benefits of the regional network, they are wary of the costs and impact on their practices. Another challenge is that in many cases, providers who traditionally have been competitors are now being asked to work together on program implementation. Largely due to financial concerns, several primary care physician practices have been recently purchased by the hospital.

EXTERNAL ENVIRONMENT

With the information systems currently serving the healthcare community, problems include disconnected islands of data, and poor coordination and limited connectivity between providers and the hospital; the lack of data often leaves clinicians and patients without needed information. Third party payors have been influential in promoting the development of an integrated information network, but they are not yet requiring participation by all providers. Because this rural region is challenged by physician recruitment, payors are reluctant to enforce such requirements.

ISSUES AND ALTERNATIVES

Working together as a team, the community physicians and the hospital can implement a community-wide health information network, but the barriers to implementation are significant. The process has stalled. Other than a small group of first adopters, physician providers are hesitant to commit the financial and practices resources necessary to embrace the network.

Options include providing additional resources to providers via the vendors or the hospital, or to change the network practice support and EMR modules completely to reduce their purchase and utilization cost.

RESTATEMENT OF DECISION SITUATION

What will the hospital and information services vendor do to work with physician practices to promote the purchase, installation, and implementation of the community health information network? The electronic health record and practice support modules have had limited adoption and implementation success. How will collaboration between players help address barriers to the vision of an integrated health information network for the entire health services area?

DISCUSSION QUESTIONS

1. Policymakers see integrated health information networks as a panacea for problems in medical services delivery, but the transition to implementation can be expensive and challenging for individual providers as well as hospital systems. What are your recommendations for the Sandhills Community Hospital and its neighboring individual practices to address the challenges of supporting a community information services network?
2. Implementing an integrated health information system requires partnerships between individuals and organizations that previously have

functioned independently. What collaborative relationships will help to ensure that the program will be successful? How can the Sandhills Health Information Network develop maximum participation and system utilization from physician groups and other ancillary providers?

3. The technology support plan for providers is critical to the success of the initiative. What collaborations will help ensure success in this area? What is the role of the relationships between the information services vendor, hospital, and providers?
4. Commitment and trust are key qualities for successful collaboration. Physicians in the community have heard that some groups are getting more financial assistance than others in purchasing and implementing the new computer system. How do such issues influence the potential for collaboration? How would you recommend the hospital address this situation?

CASE STUDY 2

Orange County Health Care Needs Assessment:

By: Pamela D. Austin, MSW, CEO, Orange County Health Needs Assessment and
Jan Frates, PhD, Professor, Health Care Administration Program at California State University Long Beach.

A Case Study in Community Outreach and Collaboration

LEARNING OBJECTIVES

After analyzing this case, the student should be able to: (list, please)

1. Distinguish between collaboration as a process and as an outcome.
2. Identify the critical success factors for collaboration.
3. Articulate the steps for a project to become an ongoing business.
4. Determine the level of investment of stakeholders in an organization's success

INTRODUCTION

Orange County, California is home to Disneyland, Knott's Berry Farm, the Angels Baseball Team, the Ducks Hockey Team, and over 3 million ethnically and socio-economically diverse people (children, adults, and families), all accessing the healthcare system with varied healthcare needs. The healthcare system is challenged to identify and prioritize the health needs of the community while simultaneously providing continuity of care, with limited resources. It is nearly impossible to accomplish these objectives without reaching out to other community partners and embracing collaboration. However, that said collaboration is often met with resistance or suspicion by the potential stakeholders themselves, who often reluctantly engage in collaborative ventures only when mandated by law or special circumstances.

> *"The argument can be made that collaboration is not a process, but the result of a process that has worked. We often focus on forming a "collaborative" before we think of moving forward toward addressing issues and accomplishing our goals. But if we focus on achieving our goals rather than on building collaboration we may find that true collaboration is much easier to achieve and sustain, becoming a far more effective process when not thought of as a primary objective.*
>
> *In reality collaboration is a natural consequence of good work and an outcome measurement of your accomplishments."*
>
> Pamela D. Austin, MSW, CEO
> Orange County Health Needs Assessment

A LITTLE HISTORY

There had been a void in Orange County for some time with respect to a coordinated effort involving healthcare providers, local government, and the community to determine and prioritize health needs. The last concerted effort dates back to the late 1970s and early 1980s through the federal health planning program (PL 93-641). The now defunct Orange County Health Planning Council (the federally designated Health Systems Agency for Orange County) did attempt to engage both healthcare providers and consumers to shape the development of Orange County's healthcare delivery system to more closely match community health needs. For a variety of reasons that were related to both the process structure and government imposed mandates, the health planning effort was not successful and formal planning ended when federal funding for the Council ceased in 1985.

A NEW COLLABORATION IMPERATIVE: SENATE BILL 697 (SB697)

The advent of the "competitive model" of healthcare delivery in the 1980s brought with it an atmosphere less conducive to collaboration. In 1994 that began to change with the passage of SB 697 (also known as the Community Benefits Law), which was sponsored by the California Association of Catholic Hospitals and the California Healthcare Association, and became effective January 1, 1995. Originally envisioned as a mechanism to measure the justification for a hospital's not-for-profit status (an IRS tax exemption classification), SB 697 became a tool of opportunity and change.

LEGISLATIVE REQUIREMENTS OF SB 697 FOR CALIFORNIA NOT-FOR-PROFIT HOSPITALS

- Reaffirm their mission statements by July 1995
- Conduct a community needs assessment every three years beginning in 1995 (1998, 2001, 2004, 2007, etc.).
- Develop and adopt a community benefits plan by April 1996, based on the results of the assessment and indicating how the identified needs would be addressed by the hospital.
- Submit a copy of the plan to the Office of Statewide Health planning and Development (OSHPD) within 150 days after the hospital's fiscal year end.
- Annually update the plan and submit updates to the State.

Purpose of SB 697 Community Benefits Planning

Community benefits planning developed as a resource to:

- work with the community to assess and respond to health needs;
- build partnerships with healthcare constituencies and stakeholders;

- contribute to building healthier communities; and
- demonstrate to the community the value of services available.

THE ORANGE COUNTY RESPONSE TO SB697

Passage of SB 697 aided in refocusing attention on identifying and addressing community health needs, and allowed for a collaborative approach to health needs identification. The health needs assessments initially produced by nonprofit hospitals were helpful for their purposes; however, they focused only on specific communities and utilized data sources and methodologies that did not allow comparison of results.

In 1997, the Hospital Association of Southern California (HASC) and the Health Care Agency (HCA) of Orange County brought a joint proposal to the local not-for-profit hospitals and formed a Community Benefits Committee, to create a collaborative process and to agree to collectively fund a county-wide health needs assessment. The proposal supported the concept of pooling resources to conduct the assessment as both effective and cost-efficient. The project would require a one year commitment and would be aimed at meeting the mandates of SB697 while also addressing the broader public health concerns of HCA. A small work group was designated in April of that same year and began designing and implementing the collaborative efforts that would later be known as the Orange County Health Needs Assessment (OCHNA).

Aligning with the Community's Needs

By early 1998, The Orange County Health Needs Assessment (OCHNA) was established as community based, not-for-profit collaborative effort, developed to carry out a countywide health assessment. It was envisioned that this effort would engender the collaboration necessary to produce an assessment that would be county-wide in scope. It also would produce consistent and reliable data that would be applicable and useful for a broad range of community healthcare providers that not only included hospitals, but community clinics, public health, and other small community-based organizations (CBOs).

This collaborative effort stands out among other similar efforts in California in a number of substantial and unique characteristics.

- Investor-owned hospitals are equal partners with the not-for-profit hospitals, although they are not required to participate under SB697.
- The County Health Care Agency is an active partner, providing both hard dollars and significant in-kind support.
- A formal project infrastructure has been defined and supported to carry out the assessment and to provide technical support to the community in use of the assessment.
- The assessment includes a population based, random digital dial (RDD) telephone survey of 5,000 Orange County households; the largest of its kind at the local level, providing first-hand (primary) data. The survey tool is modeled after the Center for Disease Control and Prevention's (CDC) Behavioral Risk Factor Surveillance Survey (BRFSS) that has been used for over 25 years across the United States to collect data on the health of the population. The survey is conducted in Spanish, English, and Vietnamese, and uses over-sampling and population weighting methodologies to ensure a representative sample of the actual population of the county. In addition, the assessment has included qualitative data in the form of community-based focus groups or smaller localized surveys to evaluate needs of hard-to-reach population subgroups such as homeless families, teens, and Hispanic day workers. The complete assessment also incorporated secondary data from national (Healthy People 2010), state (Office of State Health Planning and Development, Department of Finance), and local data provided by the Orange County Health Care Agency.
- Results of the assessment have been used in strategic planning, funding allocations, and new program development to address identified needs and priorities in the community.

ORANGE COUNTY HEALTH NEEDS ASSESSMENT (OCHNA)

Vision Statement

"Putting information into action for a healthier tomorrow."

Mission Statement

"To enhance the health and quality of life of those we serve, by putting information into action, through the support of Community Benefits

Planning (SB 697) and the provision of objective, reliable research, analysis and technical services; designed to facilitate coordination, collaboration, improve resource allocations and policy development."

Purpose and Goals

From the onset, OCHNA's primary goal was to achieve the maximum level possible of valid and reliable data that could be analyzed geographically at both the county level and by service delivery areas. These data provide information that could be used for identifying heath needs, developing priorities, designing appropriate programs, and focusing funding allocations. To this end, OCHNA is data-driven, versus agenda-motivated, with a purpose to:

- Provide objective, dependable data regarding the health and well-being of Orange County
- Highlight priorities based on the data
- Monitor progress over time
- Broadly disseminate information
- Facilitate the development of ideas and strategies
- Create institutional memory
- Be a catalyst for action

OCHNA's Benefit to the Orange County Community

- Increases collaboration with private and public community partners
- Allows participants to pool resources thereby eliminating duplicative efforts
- Provides service level data for individual partners
- Produces a comprehensive countywide needs assessment
- Access to online interactive database
- Provides a long–term strategic planning tool that identifies priority areas
- Useful for program development and capacity building
- Meets SB 697 requirements
- Reduced need for partners to have research/planning staff

Key Players: Community Partners and Steering Committee

OCHNA's infrastructure was designed to be a democratic, collaborative process that is both functional and as inclusive as possible. This objective was achieved largely through the establishment of a Steering Committee (made up mostly of appointed hospital mid-managers, whose primary responsibility was to use the data to write the SB697 community benefits reports and to develop programs that would be responsive to needs identified in through the assessment process) from community clinics and health advocates, and a broader Advisory Board referred to as the OCHNA Community Partners. The following organizations participated on one, or both, of these committees and provided the direction and oversight for OCHNA: The 26 Orange County Healthcare Association of Southern California (HASC) member hospitals; the County of Orange, Health Care Agency (also known as the Public Health Department); CalOptima (which administers the state public health insurance programs, MediCal [Medicaid] and Healthy Families [SCHIP]); Coalition of Community Clinics (22 in all); United Way of Orange County; March of Dimes and local community philanthropic foundations and advocacy groups.

Internal Situation

A critical success factor in establishing OCHNA was the commitment of initial champions, chiefly the HCA director of Public Health, and executives of the leading hospitals. Their organizations, while maintaining ownership and expressing strong support for the OCHNA mission and function, were sometimes hard pressed to maintain their funding commitments when facing budget cuts and deficits. Other area funders with a vested interest in health system assessment data displayed varying levels of commitment to OCHNA. Many stakeholders who regularly used and benefited from OCHNA's data and work provided no funding at all. Beyond the initial foundation support for the first year of operation, grant funding has remained major challenge, with only small local foundations providing any support; this is due in large part to the fact that OCHNA is a data, or research based organization, that does not provide direct health services.

OCHNA was originally structured as a collaborative project, administered by HASC. In order not to assume any financial risk if revenues failed to cover expenses, HASC developed an MOU with the County Health Care Agency (HCA) that specified that the County's contribution to the project would be used to cover personnel and administrative costs, and required that any lease agreements for office space and/or equipment be no longer than one year in length. In 2003, the County HCA went through a round of budget cuts and reduced their funding to OCHNA by 50%. Fearful that

OCHNA would not be able to raise enough money to cover the large deficit HASC gave OCHNA 90 days to raise the required funds or find a new host agency. The CEO was able gain the support needed, but HASC still did not want to remain the umbrella agency for OCHNA in a shaky fiscal environment. OCHNA proceeded to execute an agreement with Public Health Foundation Enterprises (PHFE), a 501(c)(3) nonprofit organization that provides infrastructure support and management services to a wide array of health and nonprofit organizations as their fiscal agent and sponsor. Under such arrangements, PHFE acts as employer for the staff of the not-for-profits and all funding flows through PHFE in return for a management fee, usually a set percentage of the revenues ranging from 7% to 15%. However, under this specific agreement OCHNA was invited to be a member of the Board of Directors, which would give them a direct relationship with organizations that could increase PHFE's profile and business relationships in the community. In return, PHFE waived its management fees, facilitating a mutually beneficial relationship between PHFE and OCHNA. The Community Partners transitioned from an advisory body to become OCHNA's Governing Board; their main responsibility is to provide immediate ongoing financial support and solutions for long-term stability.

OCHNA faces several operational management challenges. First, it has a very small permanent staff: the CEO, a Research/Program Coordinator, and an administrative assistant. The founding CEO has ten years of tenure in her position and is highly visible in the community; other staff have come and gone over the years. With better than average salaries for the not-for-profit field but with a heavy workload, high standards for work product, and a variable budget, it has been difficult to attract and retain qualified, capable staff who will work hard and be vested in the project. OCHNA has relied on student interns (recent Master's degree students in health and human service disciplines), who often choose to pursue an advanced graduate degree after serving two or less years with the project. Because of the cyclical and highly technical nature of its work, OCHNA contracts with consultants to conduct its surveys, but all data results are analyzed in-house by OCHNA staff as well as all report writing. Managing consultants requires a high level of skill, and must know and articulate the scope of contracted and to be able to assess the consultant's expertise. OCHNA's CEO has assembled a team of trusted technical advisors to assist her in this function.

External Situation

Initially launched with a grant from The California Endowment, OCHNA also received other donations to supplement the costs of conducting its surveys in its first five years of existence. However, its funding base was not stable. HCA, HASC member hospitals, CalOptima, and the Children and Families (First Five) Commission made consistent annual contributions, but the surveys were conducted every three years, so every third year the OCHNA's costs spiked by over 50%, resulting in a "peak and valley" fiscal trend.

Changes in funding for different segments of the Orange County healthcare system have presented both opportunities and threats. The passage of Proposition 63 in 2006 produced a new mental health revenue stream and a demand for increased attention to mental health needs. However, unlike the passage of Proposition 10 (the Tobacco Tax law requiring that these additional tax dollars be used to develop and fund programs for children under the age of six and the funding source for the First Five Commission), additional funding has not been provided to OCHNA to capture the necessary data on mental health needs of the community through the survey process, even though questions regarding those needs have been developed and included in the survey.

As with any healthcare business, OCHNA must continually reassess its business processes for continuous quality improvement, which requires constant reassessment of both data collection methods and the survey instrument. As well, OCHNA is challenged to maintain a fresh approach in the way it prepares and presents its findings.

As organizations began to use the OCHNA data, they increasingly asked OCHNA to provide additional services such as customized reports and more technical assistance to data users. While some stakeholders expressed concern that providing such services may distract OCHNA from its fundamental mission, OCHNA staff has used its expertise, capabilities, and connections to generate additional revenues out of financial necessity. Examples of such services include:

- Focus group facilitation and analysis
- Program evaluation
- Data preparation for and grant writing
- Preparation of hospitals' community benefit reports

- Continuing medical education for health care professionals
- Consulting to other communities wishing to establish health needs assessment collaboratives
- Education on the use of community health status data

ISSUES AND ALTERNATIVES

Today, OCHNA is faced with a changing hospital scene as several institutions have changed ownership and others have been publicly identified as financially fragile. Hospitals contribute approximately one third of OCHNA's funding base, so this leaves OCHNA in a highly vulnerable position. Recent and potential future changes in the HCA administrative leadership, and that organization's budget fluctuations, also make this major funder's continuing support less secure than it has been in the past. The needs assessment has become increasingly sophisticated and expensive.

OCHNA is considering the following options that will define their fate for the future:

1. Increase the scope of services and revenues by expanding the range of products and services and become a full service not-for-profit consulting organization.
2. Move away from an independent community collaborative and become a project, program or subdivision of another organization or agency.
3. Close its doors.

DISCUSSION QUESTIONS

1. What are alternative strategies for OCHNA?
2. What insights does a stakeholder analysis reveal for OCHNA? How vested are the key stakeholders in its success?

Index

Boxes, figures, and tables are indicated by *b*, *f*, and *t* following the page numbers.